# Eternity and Me
## The everlasting things in life and death

*Allan Kellehear*

**Death, Value and Meaning Series**
*Series Editor: John D. Morgan*

Baywood Publishing Company, Inc.
AMITYVILLE, NEW YORK

Published and distributed in North America by Baywood Publishing Company, Inc., 2005.

**Baywood Publishing Company, Inc.**
26 Austin Avenue
Amityville, NY 11701
(800) 638-7819
E-mail: baywood@baywood.com
Web site: baywood.com

Library of Congress Catalog Number: 2004050760
ISBN: 0-89503-298-8 (paper)

**Library of Congress Cataloging-in-Publication Data**

Kellehear, Allan, 1955-
    Eternity and me  :  the everlasting things in life and death / Allan Kellehear.
       p. cm. -- (Death, value, and meaning series)
    Originally published: Melbourne : Hill of Content, 2000.
    Includes bibliographical references and index.
    ISBN 0-89503-298-8
     1. Death. 2. Death--social aspects. 3. Death--Religious aspects. I. Title. II. Series.

BD444.K395 2004
155.9'37--dc22

                                2004050760

PUBLISHER'S NOTE: The company name Hill of Content Publishing Co Pty Ltd is no longer in existence having been taken over by Michelle Anderson Publishing Pty Ltd which is now the publisher of all titles under the former imprint.

To give light to them
  that sit in darkness
    and in the shadow of death,
      to guide our feet into the way of peace.

*Luke 1, 79*

# Contents

ഇറ

# Foreword

ℬℭ

It has been said that the world is made up not of facts, but of stories. When I first heard this as a newly minted medical academic, I was dubious . . . surely life was best defined by science with all its many techniques and tools, its power. Now, almost forty years since I received my medical degree, I find this is simply not the case. Each one of us is a story. There are certain times in life when our stories and their perspective can offer a great deal to others. Death is one such time and Allan Kellehear's compassionate and powerful stories capture the wisdom of this special time of life for all of us.

Until recently, most people's lives were not touched by death in the intimate way death touched people in the past. A hundred years ago people died at home and were buried in the back yard or very close by. These deaths involved everyone in the community. Death has not been this human for a very long time. Just **thirty** years ago, dying people were cared for in hospitals and deaths were witnessed mainly by professionals. Most people had never participated or been close to death. But death is no longer the prerogative of experts. Death is happening once again in people's homes. In their living rooms. Many more people have been with someone in the process of dying in a personal and intimate way. When death touches us like this it changes us as people and as a culture. It reminds us about what matters and who we are. It may ultimately heal us.

I have come to wonder if dying is fundamentally a reclaiming of personal integrity. Dying people are often people who have given themselves permission to be more genuine, to say things they've never said before, to become things they've never been before, because these things are simply true for them. In some way, people who are dying may give those around them that same permission for integrity. Integrity may not be a question of becoming more than we presently are, but rather letting go of the things that separate us from our wholeness. Perhaps this is why it is in times of loss that the underlying patterns of who we are may emerge most clearly.

Some years ago, I bought a little house on the top of a mountain outside of San Francisco. I've lived there for twelve years now. It was a dark old house and many of the people I first took to see it were simply appalled. One good friend in great distress asked me if I could cancel my contract and get my money back.

The house had been owned by a man who was a do-it-yourself type. Over the years he had fixed it in many different ways. If there was a hole in a wall, he took whatever board was to hand, and nailed it over the spot. If his wife wanted a door or a light fixture or a deck in a certain place, he put one there for her.

After I moved in, I began throwing these things away. I threw away light fixtures and windows and doors. I even threw away walls. And as each one of these things passed me and went out the door, I imagined I could hear my father's voice saying, "You know, that's a perfectly good window. You might need that some day." But somehow, the more I threw away, the more I had. And in the end, all that was left was what really belonged—the integrity that was innate to this particular house. Gradually the house became a container for the light and for the silence and then I painted it white. In my experience, dying can be very much like this. I have accompanied a great many people in this same process, a return to what is most fundamentally genuine in themselves.

When we begin to let go of all the ways we have been fixed by others, the ways we have fixed ourselves to make ourselves acceptable or better loved, we recover our underlying integrity. In dying, it's not windows and doors that we throw away, it's beliefs, attitudes, and ideas about what is real and what is important. Often the intensity of this movement towards integrity is so great that there is a sort of resonance between a dying person and everyone around them who is willing to be open to them and travel with them. We all move towards a great genuineness and integrity together. Being with people who are dying is painful but it can remind us of who we are and that we matter and offer us a sort of healing. It can be refuge from all that is not genuine in our society and in ourselves. It can be a place of wisdom. This is perhaps one of the best-kept secrets in our culture.

Life offers its wisdom generously. Everything teaches. But not everyone learns. This little book is a gift that gives each of us an important opportunity to learn more of life's wisdom. Each story in *Eternity and Me* is a night-light offering emotional and social guidance in our personal search for meaning in death and loss. Each story can heal us. Drawing from special moments in his own personal and professional life and the great folktales and legends of the world, Dr. Kellehear shows us that even the most difficult times can have a meaning that ultimately helps us to live more authentically. With compassion and understanding, he encourages us to be less hasty in our conclusions and remain open to surprise.

Wisdom comes most easily to those who have the courage to embrace life whole without judgment and are willing to not know, sometimes for a long time. It requires us to be more fully and simply alive than we have been taught to be. It may require us to suffer. But ultimately we will be more than we were when we began.

RACHEL NAOMI REMEN, M.D.
Author, *Kitchen Table Wisdom* &
*My Grandfather's Blessings*
Professor of Clinical Medicine, University of California
School of Medicine

# Acknowledgments

ഗ്രരു

This book grew out of a series of lunchtime discussions with my friend and colleague Bruce Rumbold. A kind and deeply spiritual person, Bruce gently encouraged my fledgling interest in writing reflective pieces about the meaning of death and loss. I am greatly indebted to Bruce for that support and stimulus. Some of my initial reflections appeared in *The Age* newspaper in Melbourne. James Button, the editor of *The Saturday Age*'s Faith column, gave me generous support and encouragement in those early days. He provided critical feedback and a rare opportunity for the general public to respond to my writing. I am indebted to him for those early days of opportunity and development.

When I began writing my reflections for this book I was influenced by the beautiful work of the physician Rachel Naomi Remen. Her best-selling *Kitchen Table Wisdom* showed me how reflective writing could be a powerful and far-reaching tool of healing for the hearts and minds of people searching for meaning in death and loss. I thank her for that lesson, for tea and story shared with me in her own kitchen in San Francisco, and for the generous foreword which appears at the beginning of this book.

I would like to give special thanks to Jan Fook, my companion in life. As a writer and academic, Jan has been a crucial influence on me through her early and long-standing interest in reflective writing. This has been an important formative influence on my own writing. Jan has also faithfully read and commented on all the chapters, and for these blessings, and her, patience in living with me in the highly distracted state in which writing them left me, I offer my heartfelt thanks.

I also extend my gratitude to Ian Anderson, Richard Bell, John Stewart, Gail Bateman, Joan Beaumont, Jon Willis, Carl Becker, Jill Henry, Alan Fettling, Glennys Howarth, Michael Ashby, Tony Magri, and my mother Tetsuko Kobayashi Kellehear. All of these people have generously shared their social or professional experiences with me. Sometimes they have also been an important part of some of my own stories.

Over the course of writing this book, I received a letter from a correspondent who wished to remain anonymous. He petitioned me to include a reflection on the problem of missing persons during my writing on loss. I am grateful for his reminder that human disappearance has a wider, and sometimes more tragic meaning than simple death. I also thank Ian Fraser for introducing me to the intriguing story of Peter Schlemihl, and my publisher Michelle Anderson for her strong belief in the social worth of this book.

For readers interested in the few references to research made in the book, critical comments concerning neurological writing about near-death experiences are supported in my earlier book *Experiences Near Death: Beyond medicine and religion,* Oxford University Press, New York, 1996; The castaway research referred to in "A History Lesson" comes from comparing the observations presented in the opening chapters of this earlier book on near-death experiences with the book about ancient mariners and castaways by Edward Leslie, *Desperate Journeys, Abandoned Souls,* Houghton Mifflin Co, Boston, 1988.

Finally, I am grateful to the many people with life-threatening illnesses who, over the course of nearly twenty years of my professional work, shared valuable time with me to discuss their diverse social and spiritual experiences.

During the meditative process of writing this book I have also drawn from a diversity of inspirational literature and retold many wonderful folktales and legends. Most of these *References* have been collected from their original sources: The story of the Buddhist nun collecting subscriptions at a crossroad is from E.T.C. Werner's, *Myths and Legends of China,* George Harrap and Co., London, 1922; The legend of the white butterfly is drawn from F. Hadland Davis, *Myths and Legends of Japan,* George Harrap and Co., London, 1912; The story about the 3 days of Bon at Yaidzu is from Lafcadio Hearn's, *In Ghostly Japan,* Charles Tuttle Co., Rutland, Vermont, 1971 (reproduced from the original 1899 edition); Henry Dore, *Researches into Chinese Superstitions,* Ch'eng-Wen Publishing, Taipei, 1966 (reproduced from the original 1914 edition).

The poem and other remarks by me about Arthur Mee concern Arthur Mee's, *The Book of Everlasting Things,* Hodder and Stoughton, London, 1927; The quotation from Aeschylus used in my piece on grief is from L. M. Savary and T. J. O'Connor (eds.), *The Heart Has Its Seasons,* Regina Press, New York, 1973; The stories about Shahrazad and the vengeful King and also the story about the man seeking his fortune in Cairo originally entitled "The Dream" are drawn from N. J. Dawood (trans.), *Tales from the Thousand and One Nights,* Penguin, Harmondsworth, 1954; The story of Le-Hev-Hev is drawn from J. L. Henderson and M. Oakes, *The Wisdom of the Serpent. The myths of death, rebirth, and resurrection,* Princeton University Press, Princeton, New Jersey, 1990.

Carl Ewald's fairytale about a fairytale is drawn from Jack Zipes (ed.), *Spells of Enchantment. The wondrous fairy tales of western culture,* Penguin, Harmondsworth, 1991; I have also referred to Anonymous *Thysia: An Elegy,* George Bell and Sons, London, 1908; Robert Fulghum, *It was on fire when I lay down on it,* Grafton Books, London, 1990; Adalbert von Chamisso, *Peter Schlemihl,* Calder and Boyars, London, 1957; The story "No Man Goes Beyond His Day" by Tomas O Crithin and Robin Flower comes from the collection by Henry Glassie (ed.), *The Penguin Book of Irish Folktales,* Penguin, Harmondsworth, 1985; Marjorie Leach, *Guide to the Gods,* ABC-CLIO, Santa Barbara, California, 1992.

The story of the Bean Boy comes from Monica Shannon's, *California Fairy Tales,* Doubleday, Page and Company, New York, 1926. The quotation from Bonhoeffer is from D. Bonhoeffer, *Letters and Papers from Prison,* SCM Press, London, 1953; The quote from Dante's Inferno is from Dante Alighieri *The Divine Comedy,* Bibliophile Books, London, 1988.

The story about Andy is drawn from "Christmas addict says no to all the trimmings," *The Saturday Age,* 5 December 1998, p. 20. Les Murray's remarks to his dying friend were reported by Philip Jones in his obituary for Mal Morgan "Love poet propelled by verse" in *The Australian,* 8 December 1999, p. 16; Comments by Caroline Jones about friendship are taken from "Faith" by Caroline Jones, *The Saturday Age,* 30 January 1999, News Extra, p. 9. The case of Greg described in my piece about sex is drawn from Melvin Morse and Paul Perry (1990), *Closer to the Light: Learning from children's near-death experiences,* Souvenir Press, London, p. 61. Gloria Stuart's story is told by Charles Laurence in the *Daily Telegraph* and reprinted as "Sex and the Sweet Old Lady" in *The Saturday Age,* 13 November 1999, p. 6. All quotations from the Bible are from the King James version.

I dedicate this book to the memory of my dear friend Doris "Folly" Hollis, and to her beloved husband, Henry Albert Edward Hollis, whom I never had the privilege to meet.

Together again. At last.

# Introduction

# The Good Story of Life

ℰᴑᴒ

When death knocks at our door, how should we answer? A long time ago, I met Susan, a forty-year-old woman who did not look a day younger than sixty. She had a cancer that would not go away and, in spreading, had robbed her body of much of its weight. The treatments, and the fatigue that accompanied them, had left her drawn and breathless. She lay on her bed with tubes coming out from her abdomen and her nose, a picture of someone in serious trouble.

As we talked, she said to me, "I'm fighting this illness, you know. That's right, isn't it? I'm doing what I can, having whatever treatments I am offered. It's so important to my family that I don't give in."

I worried that Susan felt that she was doing the "right thing" for the onlookers, especially her family, rather than for herself. Even days from her actual death she was reading books on vegan diets despite having long since given up eating solid food at all. It was not at all clear to me that "fighting" was the right choice for her. Neither of us was sure.

When you read the daily papers and listen to celebrities who have cancer, the impression you get is that "fighting" is what you are supposed to do when faced with an illness that might kill you. I saw an old movie star interviewed on TV recently who declared bravely that his intention was to "lick the cancer" that had recently returned to his body after a few years of remission. The television audience cheered madly. Clearly, he had said the right words for them. This was war.

Not long after my conversation with Susan, I met Thomas, an eighty-year-old man whose cancer was also very advanced. As we chatted, he told me that he had "made peace with his God." "I have lived a good life, done the things I wanted to do. I have some regrets—who doesn't?—but I have resigned myself to God's will. Whatever he decides about how long I will live is okay with me."

When he spoke, he appeared very calm. Here was a man with a serious cancer who had made some kind of peace deal with his fate.

But it was not clear to me then that "making peace" was the best thing for him or for his family. Although Thomas appeared to be at peace with himself, some of his family confided in me that they thought he might have "given up." They needed some sign that he *wanted* to live. Making peace didn't really fit the bill.

But do war and peace exhaust our repertoire of responses to something that threatens to kill us? Are fighting or surrendering the sum total of our choices? The Jedi Knight, Obi-Wan Kenobi, observed wisely in a scene from the film *Star Wars* that there are more ways to deal with trouble than fighting. And he is right.

In *The Arabian Nights,* a king who witnesses too much infidelity among women, including his own wife, decides to sleep with a new woman every night and kill her in the morning. As the virgin women in his kingdom die, all parents with daughters become increasingly gripped by fear. In a bid to stop the killings, Shahrazad, the eldest daughter of the king's most senior public official, offers herself to him. With the king's consent, she arranges for her youngest sister Dinarzad to sleep under his bed so that when he has had his way with her she may bid her farewell before morning.

Unbeknown to the King however, Shahrazad has arranged for her sister to ask her to tell her a story to while away the hours.

The arrangements go as planned, and Shahrazad begins her tale but fails to complete it. So that he can hear the ending, the king gives Shahrazad a reprieve from death and arranges for her to come to his bed the next night to make love and to hear the end of the story.

This she does and, when it is over, she begins a new story to fill in the remaining time. This one is also interrupted by the dawn and so night after night—for a thousand and one nights—Shahrazad extends her own life and those of all the virgin women in the kingdom. Eventually she bears children for the king and he ends his serial revenge on womanhood.

Shahrazad lives not by fighting the king or resigning herself to her fate, but by engaging the heart and mind of that which might kill her. Eventually she lives for more than a thousand and one nights. She tells stories, each one designed for one night only, to allow her to live until the next day—not forever, not for eleven nights, or a hundred; not even for a thousand and one nights. Eventually, of course, Shahrazad dies, probably of old age, but it is not the king's wrath that kills her.

We see this all the time in people who seem to be very close to dying but don't die. Instead they live on to have an important role in the story of their last Christmas, or their daughter's birthday, or that special visit from an old friend. We see it in people who battle on with serious heart disease or a cancer that never seems to go away and, then, while working on other plans, eventually die of something else all together.

The stories we tell ourselves are central to our lives because they give them purpose and meaning. Although we must all do what is necessary to live, and sometimes this might mean being a fighter or a peacemaker, necessity does not make us *want* to live. All of us live through our own stories, and to go on living we must continue to tell them—the big ones: The best dad in history; The woman who made a difference to others; The boy who knew too much; The girl who loved cats; The family that planted trees; or The woman who told her illness who was in charge of her appointment diary. These are the stories worth living for, the stories that MAKE us live. They do not protect us from death or loss, because no story can do that but, as Shahrazad has taught us in *The Arabian Nights,* a story can make our day. And a day at a time is all we need.

The chapters in this book are forged from some of my own and other people's stories. Some are woven from some of the world's great folktales and legends. I have shared them with people living in the shadow of death. And I share them with you in the same spirit.

Some day we will all die. But in the meantime, you can offer Death this warning: as Shahrazad is my witness, good stories can take a long time to tell.

# When death knocks
# at our door . . .

# 1

# The Tree of Life

## ℘ℂℜ

When faced with a life-threatening illness, most people want to be told the truth. What do they mean? Often they want answers to questions about how critical their illness is and how long they have to live. These questions are difficult to answer. And the answers can be misleading. The effect can often be depressing and unhelpful. But from time to time, you learn some kinds of truths from them.

I was recently told of a variation of an O. Henry short story about winter leaves and life and death. In this case, though, the story was true. A medical colleague who came to speak to me after a talk I had given at his hospital related this case to me. Some years ago, he was looking after a woman suffering from an advanced cancer. His patient asked how long she might live. He mentioned his reservations about making predictions, but she continued to press him for some kind of answer. In the end, he poetically suggested that she might live to see autumn.

At that point she gazed through the window of his surgery and, motioning towards the deciduous tree growing there, said, "So when the last leaf on that tree drops to the ground, I shall be gone." He was surprised by her observation and speechless.

When his patient had left the room, my colleague became worried that such symbolism might become a self-fulfilling prophecy. He immediately went outside with a small piece of wire and attached one of the leaves to its branch. Autumn came and went and, as the months passed, the woman returned to the doctor's office. She was doing better than expected and her treatments were to continue, he told her.

· After this news, the woman left the room and walked around the building to inspect the tree outside his room. It now stood almost completely bare except for the solitary leaf, which seemed to hang on despite the winter winds. The doctor held his breath.

Slowly the woman walked to the tree, her eyes moving to the lone leaf. She stepped forward and took the leaf in her hand and inspected this warrior more closely. A second or two passed and she began to laugh out loud. Autumn had come and gone, but she and her "leaf" had steadfastly remained despite their mutually difficult circumstances. Uncertainty had triumphed over prediction yet again. And that victory was a celebration of her doctor's compassion and her ability to live against the odds. Whatever her mind had understood by her doctor's earlier forecast, she had failed to realize that her own courage recognized no seasons.

The story in the Book of Genesis is also about trees and truth-telling. Adam and Eve were forbidden to eat from the Tree of Knowledge of Good and Evil. Despite this injunction Eve, and then Adam, ate from the tree and so their troubles began. The lesson, that knowing is not always helpful, is an old one.

When the ancient Greeks spoke about truth, they used the word *aletheia,* which means "discovery." Similarly emphasizing the idea of truth as "discovery," the poet Ortega y Gasset used the image "to take away the veil that covers and hides a thing." Medical predictions about life expectancy rarely "take away the veil," but what they hide, in their turn, is priceless.

Pronouncements about longevity can obscure from you your own qualities of courage, determination and hope; your body's ability to endure, survive, and respond to healing; and your doctor's hopes and skills in helping you to harness both. The truth behind the story of the woman, her doctor and the one-leaf tree is the one she saw in the tied-on leaf and not in the poetic prediction she had heard the year before.

After Adam and Eve ate from the Tree of Knowledge, they were barred from the Garden of Eden and the resources of another tree—the Tree of Life. They chose knowledge over eternal life, and in the process enrolled us all in death.

But let us not repeat their mistake of equating "knowing" with "living." Being told that you might have only a certain number of months to live is about as useful as knowing that you are naked in the Garden of Eden when there is only one other human being on the planet who would notice. No one, including medical experts, can give you an appointment with death. Only life organizes that kind of appointment. And only you can decide to be late for it.

# 2

# Fear and Dread

ഇൗൽ

Do I fear death? Freud once said that man could no more look at the sun than imagine his own death. I have tried to imagine my own death many times. I have sat with people near death. I have gazed at death in the morgue and inside anatomy labs. And I have read a lot about death.

At the end of life, the journey of death must be understood as an experience. We may argue about the destination of the journey but it is a journey nonetheless. Do I fear the journey then?

Like many people, I fear separation from the people I love. I am intimidated by the prospect of a journey with an unclear ending. And I don't much relish going on the journey alone. I have made several modest but reluctant journeys before, some when very ill and others, like the one I will retell here, when I was well, minding my own business, and blissfully ignorant of any looming trouble.

I once lived in a small rural town called Coolamon, about a half-hour drive outside of Wagga Wagga in New South Wales, and at that time, home to about a thousand people. Once a week I would go to art classes in Ganmain, the next, smaller town with only a few hundred residents. The art classes were held in the local primary school around seven on a Thursday night.

I came home from work, ate an early dinner, got in the car and headed down a dead-straight road that ran along an old rail line. The road had only one kink in it, one small bend, which skirted around a couple of tall wheat silos by the rail line. Aside from that brief diversion, the road ran true for miles, with the rail line on one side and an endless horizon of wheat fields on the other. The road to Ganmain was also flat as flat could be. You could see for miles.

One hot Thursday evening, at the height of summer, I got in the car as usual to go to my classes. I drove down into the town's only major intersection, turned left, and headed out along the Ganmain road as always.

As the car made its way along the road, I saw something that no city boy from Sydney had ever seen before. Coming across from my right-hand were gigantic grey and purple thunderstorm clouds. They were tall and capped white on their rapidly unfolding plumes. Gazing at them for a moment I saw flashes of lightning. Below the flattened grey body of their darkest edges was rain. And below that was a wind as wild as the devil's own horses. But that was not all.

On the left-hand side of my vision, also heading for me along that lonely road, was a tall and angry wall of red dirt that rose sharply into the skies—a dust storm. I had only ever seen one of these before, in Bathurst many years ago and, unlike this one, it traveled unaccompanied. This one was like a wall the size of a small skyscraper and about a mile or two across. It was visually impenetrable and its colors changed back and forth from bright orange to red as it swallowed up the wheat fields beneath its path. When it passed a tree, fence or outbuilding each of them simply disappeared. There was no doubt about it. Both the dust and thunderstorm were going to meet, and it was quite apparent to me that this marriage was going to occur over the fast disappearing stretch of road I was traveling on. The weather advanced so rapidly that, before I knew it, my car was about to plunge headlong into these colliding systems.

I had never liked thunderstorms. When they came, I preferred to be indoors. They seared me as a child, and I never felt comfortable about them as an adult. Every year people are zapped by lightning. Sometimes these are golfers; at other times they are people just walking home from school or work. If I go, I'd rather not go with a bang and a sizzle, thank you.

As for dust storms, this misty wall of red and choking dust didn't seem to have much room for oxygen, and this image did not make me feel any cheerier. At the time, it all happened so quickly that I could not say that I consciously felt fear. But the violence before me, the lack of any warning, the isolation I felt in confronting this force of nature, and the complete unfamiliarity of the situation, made me feel stressed, vulnerable and intimidated.

What happened?

As the car entered the storms, normal vision outside the car windshield disappeared. I stopped the car—right there—smack in the middle of the road. I had no choice. Anyone who could subsequently drive far enough into this situation so as to collide with my stationary car was obviously driving by radar and not human vision, and if they had radar they would be able to avoid me. The car bobbed about with the pushy force of the turbulence. All I could see was swirling orange and purple. From time to time there were flashes of bright yellow and silver light. There were sounds of exploding thunder, but the wind around the crevices of the car produced strangely melodic, siren-like sounds—cries and high-pitched whistles. The scene became psychedelic, beautiful.

Some moments passed. I don't know how many. During that time, the light and sound show, seen and heard from the bubble of my automobile, was like nothing I had ever experienced. It was both frightening and beautiful, a feast for the eyes and the ears, but also for the soul. It was a magnificent display and a totally enveloping one.

And then, something happened which, at the time, seemed equally remarkable. Opening up before me, at first unrecognizable, because I had adjusted to the surreal and unusual, was the old road before me. At first I could see just a few feet of it ahead of me and then, a moment later, a few feet more. In almost a trance, I put the car into gear and slowly resumed my trip along the road. In a short space of time, I emerged again on the road into a more conventional thunder and rainstorm. The confusion of the collision had passed, and I could see again. And then I arrived in Ganmain—for my art lessons.

Do I fear death? Yes, I think I do. I would rather be well than sick. I would rather be sick than dead. As we say in Australia, I wouldn't be dead for dollars. But die I will. Eventually. I'll come home from work one day, or maybe I'll be on holidays or in retirement, about to embark on or plan some activity. I'll travel suddenly into some social or medical emergency. And, as I look up and into the road ahead, something unexpected will cross my path. I will not like the look of it. I will grip the steering wheel of my life tightly, and I will take a deep breath and wonder about the outcome.

I will dread the day. All I can hope is that the journey is unexpectantly surprising, even wondrous. And that at the end of the journey, just a short distance from where I am looking, the old road will re-appear before me.

# 3

# Friendship

৪০৫৪

I once conducted a social study on what happens to people when they develop a serious cancer for which a medical prospect of cure was unlikely. One of the things that I expected to find was a high level of social rejection—people in this situation might lose friends and partners for fear of "catching" the cancer. Nothing could be further from the truth. Out of a hundred people I interviewed, about eighty reported no change, particularly in their close friendships and family relations.

A few people did report rejecting social experiences. A husband suddenly left his ill wife. Adult sisters told a sibling not to tell others that she had cancer because of the "shame" involved. But these were uncommon if sad exceptions. Most people reported developing closer bonds with their friends or finding new ones. For everyone, the comfort of friends was important. In illness, as in the rest of life, it is not always clear where these friends come from. But come they do, and often from unexpected quarters. All of a sudden, you have a new friend for life.

The Australian broadcaster Caroline Jones observed that "at its deepest level, friendship is the meeting of kindred spirits, that gracious encounter where my loneliness is relieved in the most profound way . . . my suffering has been comforted in the empathic presence of a friend." And she is right. I think of friends, and the arrival of new ones, as a kind of social miracle, an inexplicably wondrous thing.

When I arrived at my sixth new primary school, I had no friends for the first three days. They were long days. On the fourth day, I observed a soccer game in the schoolyard. I asked if I could join in. I was directed to the boy who owned the ball. This boy said, no, I could not join them—he had "enough" players. I sat despondently on the sidelines, and soon became annoyed. At other schools I had been a good soccer player. Once I had the ball between my feet, for example, it was usually quite a task to take it away from me.

I darted into the crowd of boys, stole the ball away and began "dribbling" it across the schoolyard to the cries and howls of the players. When I was surrounded, I left the ball and ran clear. When the game resumed, I began this private nonsense all over again. On my third run, one of the players grabbed me and hauled me against a nearby wall (regrettably, I was a small skinny child). As he threatened to send me to Jesus for a face-to-face encounter, a large tough-looking boy slipped between my interlocutor and me. I still remember the words of that boy: "If you want to take him out, you have to take me out first."

I was released in more ways than one. In that moment, Tony became my friend. I don't know where he came from. He was nothing like me in build, and not the kind of person whose eyes I would meet if I were walking in a new neighborhood. But here he was—a friend.

He joined me in subsequent forays into the "main" soccer game. With Tony beside me, no one dared to threaten me again.

We were joined by a third, and then a fourth and fifth boy. Soon we were all "invited" to join the main game, and I settled into my new school. Tony is still one of my dearest friends.

Who can say from where friends may come? And though we may not know from where, we do know that their power is in their connection with your own spirit, their joining together in your experience, the buoyancy of their love and support. In the darkest moments of life, their communion, for it is a communion—a joining in faith—is a crucial aid in the ability to face the things that threaten you, exclude you, diminish you.

If love is there in the valley of the shadow of death, that love is there in the shape of friends. In this way, as the composer Benjamin Godard once wrote, angels do guard thee.

# 4

# The Question

భెఁ౯

In my time working in death, dying and palliative care, there is one question I am asked again and again. Children ask me. Adults ask me, some of them in half whispers. And a few months ago, I had the distinct impression that one of my dogs asked me when I was burying her companion of ten years. They all ask: When beings die, do they somehow live on?

If ever there was a question designed to test you, this must surely be it. Skeptics watch to see if you will "weaken" and open yourself to traditional religious views or New Age fairy floss. Their eyes narrow if you start talking about near-death experiences. My friends in the church wait to see if there is some hope for me, as someone who might understand that religious traditions are living ones, designed for hope and faith, even in these modern times.

But the eyes I care most about, and the ones most steady on my own, are those that belong to my inquirer. These questions do not arise from intellectual curiosity or the desire to test me, but from a personal encounter with death. Sometimes people ask me because they mourn the loss of someone they loved. Sometimes they ask because *they* are looking death in the face. The questions are sometimes motivated by their fear of death, and my arrival at a party, dinner or public function gives them the chance to scratch at that fear in relative anonymity.

But what a question to ask. I often wondered how priests and ministers replied. I used to think they would find it easy. They could turn to the Bible and embellish a passage they found there. Or perhaps their denomination had comforting pictures of the afterlife. Later I teamed that the Bible has very little to say about the afterlife. Some Christian religions even hold beliefs similar to the materialists claiming that when we die we turn to worm fodder, at least until Christ's Second Coming, when the trumpets blown on that great occasion literally wake up the dead.

But not all questions can be answered in words. To begin to think about this reminds me of the saying, "Talking about music is like dancing about architecture." And so the question about whether people live on when they seem to die may be like many other questions such as: How did the music affect you? How deep are my personal losses? How do I love thee?

Questions such as these do not have yes or no answers because they are questions about meanings. And the best replies to most questions of purpose and meaning are rarely found in words. Sometimes only experiences can help you. Sometimes in the act of remembering, for example, I can feel the outline and depth of my regrets and losses, although I express these to no one. Sometimes in the act of sitting alone listening to music, I can find hope again, at least for tomorrow. Sometimes when I look at a photo of those I love, I can begin to list in my heart all the ways that I love them, and then think of a new way to show them.

In these ways, sorting through old memories or experiences as diverse as past losses, unusual dreams, or old arguments may help you find your answer, one that will satisfy *you*. Time will bring you that reply because that is one of its purposes. Only prejudice—a made-up mind—will thwart that slow, gentle and inevitable unveiling of private meaning, which comes from looking again at your life experiences through a different set of questions. Like all learning that is worth the effort, be patient. And be prepared to be surprised.

# 5

# Near–Death Experiences

୫⃝୧

When people who become unconscious during a heart attack or some other illness are revived, some of them report unusual experiences. Some say that they have had an out-of-body experience during which they witnessed their own resuscitation. Some report traveling down a dark tunnel only to appear at a rural scene of bliss and beauty. Once there some people meet a bright being of light and undergo a review of their past lives. Others report meeting deceased relatives or friends.

Most report feeling wonderful and describe their experiences as real as anything they have encountered—their experiences are not dreamlike or hallucinatory in quality. The name commonly attached to these cases is near-death experiences.

In group discussions with people living with cancer, I am frequently asked about near-death experiences. Commonly, the questions are skeptical, something like, aren't near-death experiences all really so much nonsense? Or, aren't near-death experiences really so much New Age fluff? Or even, are we silly to believe in them as some kind of evidence for life after death? The neuroscientists have got this kind of experience explained these days, haven't they?

It seems that after a decade or so of being flooded with TV and magazine features on near-death experiences some people feel cynical. We've just mapped the human gene, so why can't we explain near-death experiences? But it appears that mapping genes is easy streets compared to understanding near-death experiences. Let me explain.

At a weekend lunch with some psychiatrist friends one afternoon, I related some of these stories. They laughed and looked knowingly at each other. They told me how these "experiences" were electrical disturbances of the brain brought on by an oxygen crisis near death. I asked them for some evidence, perhaps something they had read in a respected journal article or book. They couldn't give me any.

Now, unlike Winnie the Pooh, I am not a "bear with a little brain." I am all for the idea of a fair and decent explanation for anything. I am prepared to accept the idea of hallucinations— ones associated with drugs, organic brain disorders, certain types of mental illness, or even those associated with toxic bodily processes near death. Just give me a reference so that I can see the evidence for myself.

Eventually I chased up the articles and found that most of the neurological writing on near-death experiences is only specu- lation. It appears that many writers in the area exaggerate. Some authors, for example, cite "other studies" to back up their claims, but when you follow them up they are not studies at all, or they are articles which, in their turn, cite articles that are speculative rather than real, or misinterpret the studies badly, or do both. Other articles conveniently leave out studies or arguments that do not fit the author's theory of hallucination or model of consciousness. There seems to be a significant amount of unreliable writing about near-death experiences, and much of the writing that does appear to be reasonable is only speculation.

In itself this is not a difficulty. Good speculation is called theory and good theory can guide careful observations on their way to establishing facts. But speculation about neurology is not the problem but the speculation over the connection between sensations and the experiences responsible for them. In other words, if science discovered the physical processes responsible for the *sensations*, it could make claims about the *experience*. This is like maintaining that if we can identify the physiology behind smiling, laughing, and feelings of contentment, we can understand happiness. This is leg-pulling country. Is there modesty, or even caution in this logic? I think not.

I do not know if near-death experiences are good evidence of survival. But I am curious about them, and I am happy to stay that way. I do not believe that neuroscience can resolve problems that are fundamentally philosophical, or that philosophical questions can address theological ones.

What I like about religious people is that they are honest enough to declare an interest. Skeptics often hide their hand under the guise of scientific neutrality and clearly this is an area where "neutrality" of any sort is difficult for all parties.

For those who wonder whether their dead loved ones have survived, or even whether they can look forward to life beyond death, the real answers must be couched in terms of possibilities. Since we know only a small part of what happens when we die, philosophically and medically, the possibilities are significant. Even if we knew all about the physiology of the dying brain, the possibility of human survival could not be ruled out. It does not follow that the physiological basis of life is life itself. A radio, for example, is not music, however necessary having the former might be to the enjoyment of the latter.

A fair observation to make under the circumstances must be that uncertainty continues to be a sound and reasonable basis for hope. If you hope that life is possible beyond death, the near-death experience offers some fertile and thought-provoking imagery. In this sense, the physical appearance of death may be deceptive.

On the other hand, if you hope that survival is not possible, it will be important to hold tightly to the idea that physiology is consciousness. The end of one is the end of the other. In other words, what you see is what you get. Well, that is more than can be said about the professional literature on the subject. And that's comforting isn't it? Because if someone must have the final say about the chances of survival beyond death, it's good to know that it is still *you*.

# 6

# The Body

ഇൗൽ

There are several books on the market describing what death is like. They make grim reading. None of them spares you any of the gruesome details. Breathlessness is breathlessly described. Nausea is explained *ad nauseam*. Pain and convulsions are sketched in agonizing detail. Every little bit, and then some. These books are the roller-coaster rides of death and dying. You open the book, strap yourself in, read the first chapter, brace yourself and then, weeeeee—chariot ride through a set of anatomical images that make the Marquis de Sade look like he needs assertiveness training.

But are we any better off? Do these books tell us what death is really like?

When I was seventeen, I was involved in a car accident. Three of us decided to go out to get burgers at midnight one Saturday. We got as far as four blocks from the house when a car, driven by a woman rushing home to her children, hit us. A man walking his dogs saw the accident. He said that her car hit ours on the passenger side. She was speeding. Our car rolled once and then the tires peeled off as the wheel rims dug into the asphalt. As the rims gouged the road, the car flipped into the air and sailed into a telegraph pole. It wrapped itself around the pole and slid to the ground with a resounding crash. The engine of the woman's car was ejected by the impact of the collision and lay several meters away from the crash site.

What happened inside our car?

When the other car hit us, we were talking, but I don't remember the topic. I caught a glimpse of headlights. There was a bang, which stopped the conversation. We tamed upside down. I raised my arm above my head to protect myself against my fall on the car's ceiling as we rolled. I smelt dust in my nostrils. There was another loud explosion, and I felt jerked about and dropped. Dust and glass went everywhere. As the car stopped, I turned to the friend who was driving and remarked that this meant hamburgers were out of the question. The accident gave me a broken pelvis.

To onlookers, the incident looked far worse than my recollection of it. To me, it was much like rolling down a hill in a potato sack with someone malting violent banging noises as I went. I would have been more scared if I had been the witness walking his dogs.

The sports commentator at a racetrack can describe a fall or a crash in the way the crowds see it but not as the driver or rider suffers it.

My experience of the crash was no fun, let me tell you, but it was a long way from the dramatic eyewitness account I heard later. Both were "true" accounts, but they came from different perspectives. The witness's account reported what our crash was like for onlookers. My account told how it felt for me, an insider.

At a dinner, party one night, my mother's chair collapsed, for no apparent reason. We rushed to her side, but she was unconscious. Slowly she came around and asked what had happened. To us, she was there one minute and gone the next, in a jerky set of movements that ended with a crashing noise on the floor. It was dramatic and scary. Everyone was shocked and distressed.

When my mother had recovered sufficiently, she recalled the conversation, a sudden inexplicable movement to one side and then blackness. Even in this murkiness, however, she recalled feelings of comfort and peace, as if she were having a good sleep. She was better off than her panicking hosts and guests.

When doctors describe someone fainting, their descriptions will be about the effects of heat, or standing too long, or cardiac insufficiency, or fluid dynamics, or the psychosomatics of threat and shock.

Ask someone who has fainted what it was like, and their account will sound like a page out of *Alice in Wonderland,* or my mother's story of a dark and velvet place of peace.

When it comes to death, remember that few people know what dying is really like, least of all those who have not done it. Very old people often say that they feel middle-aged or younger. People who have been resuscitated consistently report pleasant feelings. Those who recover from a coma often report dreamy or dreamless sleepy states. The worst rumors about death seem to come from people with the least first-hand experience. Isn't that always the way?

# 7

# Sex

ಬಿಂಚಿ

It was eight in the evening, and I had just finished a late dinner when the phone rang. David was a mature-age student I had taught several years earlier. He had remembered that I had a special interest in death and dying and called me in a moment of need to talk to someone who felt comfortable with death.

His son, a seventeen-year-old in his final year of school, had come home one evening complaining of back pain. The next day his son went to see his local doctor and was referred to a specialist. After several tests, this young man was found to have a very aggressive form of cancer. He was not expected to live more than a few weeks.

David and I rehearsed a lot of his concerns over the phone that night, but I always remember his tender, if shy, regrets about his son's lack of sexual experience. He felt, and rightly, that sexual experience was one of the great joys of life, and he expressed his sorrow that his son might not now have the chance to enjoy that gift.

This was not the first time that sex had entered into my conversations with people who lived with critical illness, or their carers. I have had many talks with men and women, hetero-sexuals and same sex attracted people, about their sexual needs while living with cancer or HIV. If they are not depressed, recent weight loss and a positive attitude can make them feel quite sexy. Their interest in sex can increase. For some, this is part of embracing life. On the other hand, it may be a reaction to fears of abandonment. For others, it may be a simple response to improved health as they become more conscious of diet, exercise, and relaxation.

Interest in sex among people who are ill does not always express itself in all its usual ways. Sometimes, vaginal thrush or dryness from different forms of cancer therapy may make intercourse unpleasant for women. This is common and may preclude all sexual relations. Sometimes, however, sexual intimacy continues, expressing itself, for instance, in time spent naked together, caressing each other in bed. There is more to sex than intercourse, as we are often reminded, and much more to love than sex. And so it is for many couples. Physical intimacy knows diversity of expression well. Teenagers of every generation know this wisdom. Sometimes we learn the old ways again.

Once, in a hospice, after I had spent time talking to a woman in her seventies, the ward nurse took me to task for discussing sex with an old lady, as she put it. She said that such con-versations were "intrusive." The assumption that old people have sex was "disgusting." Anyway, she declared, the woman to whom I spoke was single (!).

But older people do enjoy sex. Sometimes they are self-conscious about their sexual desires, especially in the face of community prejudice about sex and old people.

Sex is not about age but physical attraction and the exchange of affections. The only requirements here are imagination and willingness. You don't lose either with age.

We often unconsciously identify sex with life, its creation, and joy. Not many people associate sex with aging and dying. But they are part of a whole person and wholly a part of their activities, desires, and choices. Poor health may interfere with sexual desire, but it is not inevitable. Sexual feelings are natural for everyone, including those living with critical illnesses, the aging, and those near death because, among other things, they are *not dead yet*.

The American physician Melvin Morse reported the story of Greg, a thirteen-year-old boy dying of cystic fibrosis. Several weeks before he died, Greg reported visions during his waking hours. They were pleasant and contained visitors, including God. It was not easy for Greg to distinguish between reality and visions, but Morse reports one poignant clue. In his visions, Greg was able to achieve erection and orgasm. In reality, because of the severity of his disease, neither was possible.

I recounted Greg's story to David. I do not know whether Greg imagined or enjoyed sex in another reality, but I do know that unexpected things happen near death, as in the rest of life, and that includes sexual experiences.

David could not know whether his son had or had not enjoyed satisfying sexual experiences before or after his illness. But we do know that between sex and love, love is certainly greater. And if David's love for his son was anything to go by, his son had drunk deeply from that well and so David had little to worry about and much to be proud of. Can anyone ask for more?

# 8

# The Burden of
# Peter Schlemihl

ℰℐℛℛ

There is a wonderful German story about a man who came unstuck in life by selling his shadow. Tucked beneath this story is another about how his friends coped with the burden of his miseries.

Peter Schlemihl sold his shadow, the symbol of his social identity, for a magical purse that became a never-ending source of gold coins. At first delighted that he had traded something of minor importance for something of immeasurable value, Peter Schlemihl found himself a social pariah.

Within minutes of doing the deal—with a sinister-looking but deferent old man in a grey suit—Peter found that children laughed and mocked him. To adults who saw this strange, shadowless man, Peter became an object of pity or fear. He learned quickly that he needed to control his physical and social environment if he was to avoid continuous public curiosity and derision.

Peter hired and later befriended a servant named Bendel, who looked after his affairs, arranging transport, social functions, and payments, even creating elaborate social and physical deceptions. He listened to Peter's woes and cries of self-pity for hours on end. Long-suffering and devoted, Bendel would arrange the lights at functions so that no one attending them looked as if they had shadows. In the sunlight, Bendel walked closely by his master, strategically maneuvering around Peter to give the impression of overlapping shadows. Nothing was too much trouble for Bendel.

It soon became apparent that Peter Schlemihl could not go on like this forever, and he quickly regretted his decision to sell his shadow for a magic purse.

He remembered that the man in grey would come by and visit him a year from the date of the original deal. The task for Peter was to survive that year, at the end of which he could exchange his purse for his old shadow.

In the meantime, Peter and Bendel moved to another province where Peter was not known. In this place, Peter quickly became important, many thinking that he was the King of Prussia traveling *incognito*.

Here, he soon met and fell in love with Mina, the beautiful daughter of a game warden. They were besotted with each other, but Peter withheld his secret about his shadow from her. He hoped that in a year it would be resolved and that he and Mina would marry.

The man in the suit came at the arranged time, but the news was not good. He insisted that Peter should keep the purse and receive his shadow back as long as he signed over his soul— to be collected on Peter's death. Having made one mistake, Peter was not going for this deal on any account. Misery then heaped on misery.

Mina was not allowed to marry Peter and was quickly betrothed, against her will, to a morally suspect suitor. Peter's house was subsequently demolished by rioting crowds who had heard of the scandal. Bendel attempted to attack the man in the grey suit and wrestle his master's shadow off the scoundrel, but to no avail.

Both sat depressed at the end of these traumatic affairs. Afterwards, Peter insisted that his servant leave him. In gratitude, Peter gave Bendel a substantial amount of money to use as he pleased. From this time on, Peter Schlemihl wandered the earth, a solitary figure with only his dog Figaro for company.

Many years later, Peter fell ill and was cared for in a public institution for the socially dejected. One day, he overheard a conversation between a kind man and a beautiful widow, whom he soon knew were Bendel and Mina. They did not recognize him because he had grown old, his hair disheveled and overgrown. Bendel and Mina spoke about why they performed this caring work after having experienced so much of their own suffering.

It was a poignant moment for Peter Schlemihl who realized that much goodness and wisdom could come from adversity and suffering, both his own and other people's.

Peter Schlemihl's story is not one about the consequences of foolishness but rather how imperfections in life may create fertile grounds for moral and spiritual improvement. When we read Peter's story, we follow the development of qualities of humility, sensitivity, kindness, and personal and social insight forged from personal pain and loss. Peter has moved a long way from his shallow, self-absorbed and egocentric life.

Peter's development paralleled those of Bendel and Mina. Although Peter's suffering was a burden to them, it was by virtue of those very difficulties that Bendel and Mina were able to see beyond the confines of their limitations. They had been ill-prepared for Peter's predicament.

Pain is difficult. And depending on others can be difficult, even irksome, too. The multiple losses in dying, like a mystery well, seem to have no bottom. All this can force us to see other people's suffering more clearly, encouraging us to relieve our carers of the burden that we seem to be imposing on them. The shadows that we cast are important to others. And they are not ours to sell to whoever will buy. As Peter Schlemihl and his friends discovered, good things may come from tragedy and adversity. War veterans, prisoners of war, and survivors of tragedies know this well. At the end of life, this may be the final and most unexpected gift of all.

# 9

# Christmas with Andy

ଚ୍ଚୁ

For most of my childhood, I considered Christmas to be a rather dull affair. All our friends were with their relatives, but the only family we had did not live in Australia. At seventeen, I got fed up with these desultory Christmases and decided on some reorganization. Mum didn't work on Christmas Eve and most of my friends were either at a loose end or out at parties. I decided to become one of those parties. I asked my friends to meet me at Midnight Mass on Christmas Eve and to come back to my place afterwards. I went out and bought a "live" Christmas tree—the biggest one I could find.

Mum decorated it until it looked like something out of a nineteenth-century English Christmas card. After Mass we all opened our gifts at my place and ate and drank together. Mum put on a record, which played all night—Bing Crosby's album called "White Christmas." In a surreal way, we all loved it and took turns replaying it. At last I found myself looking forward to Christmas.

I never thought much about this until last year when I read the story of Andy Park of Melksham, in Wiltshire, England. Andy was described in the newspaper as a "yuletide addict." He had eaten Christmas dinner with all the trimmings every day for the past five years. He had grown to 101 kilograms.

Every night Andy packs three presents for himself and puts them under his tree. He spends thousands of dollars a year on food, decorations, gifts, and fairy lights. He consumes hundreds of turkeys, sweets, and puddings annually.

Andy says he began doing this five years ago "to cheer himself up." He always tries to invite people over to help him celebrate each day because "it makes life far less dull."

In the light of my story, you can see what I am about to say. I like Andy. I don't think he is a "yuletide addict." I don't think he is a freak, as the newspaper would have us believe. Yes, Andy has a weight problem, but he is not alone in that. You and I are reading about Andy because he has found a way to make his life more meaningful, happier, and is able to spread that around a bit. He has what psychologists call "agency"— an ability to feel he has some control, however modest, over the fate of his life. Other people who can't make their own Christmases might, unbeknown to you, appear as premature entries in the obituary columns or in anonymous statistics for depression. Andy is not going to be among them. Andy is a man of action.

Sometimes life doesn't play the tune for you that it seems to play so effortlessly for other people. You hate your job, or you can't get one. Your third marriage looks like it is going the way of your first and second. When you walk out of the doctor's surgery with your diagnosis of cancer or HIV, past all the patients with coughs and colds, you wonder why you couldn't have been one of them—instead of the person with the life-threatening condition. Sometimes, as the saying goes, trouble just happens. The question is: what are you going to do about it?

I am often amazed at how colleagues in the health professions shake their heads at the news of someone flying off to foreign lands in search of quack cures. "They spend their life's savings on charlatans and fraud contraptions," they lament. And it's true, many do. That is part of the sadness of personal troubles. People do desperate things at desperate times. But another side of the story is that, in the absence of anything tangible that we can offer, people are entitled to seek hope and meaning in any way they see fit. Yes, they are vulnerable. But they are not stupid or freaks because they will not just sit and accept their lot.

To break with convention, to refuse to accept your lot if it seems dull, unfair, or tragic, is to regain some measure of dignity in and control over your life. It is also to break from the pack and risk not only failure and derision, but also the prospect of success. You become like Andy—a bright and genuine possibility for your own happiness.

# 10

# Joy

ॐ

What is "Joy" asked a colleague who left the room without waiting for an answer.

But I know what joy is. It's an old-fashioned term that mainly appears on Christmas cards these days, but it's a good word for a good experience. And it's an excellent topic to talk about, swap stories on, to alert yourself to the all-important question: are you getting enough of it?

Think about it for a moment. If there aren't enough—or any—joyful moments in your life, maybe there is a message there for you, such as, Go back! You're going the wrong way.

When I turned twelve, I wanted to do something special for my birthday. I decided I would go fishing to see if I could get "lucky" . . . I got up at four in the morning, crawled into my clothes, grabbed the fishing gear and left the house to walk alone in the cold and dark toward the railway station. In thirty minutes, I had caught the train to Como station and was walking down toward the end of Como pier beside the George's River in Sydney's south side. I cast my line into the water and waited.

I had caught a lot of fish in my time, although for some reason they were all pretty small despite being mostly legal size. Some men once told me that my tackle was too small—the hooks I used were too small—and that's why I never caught anything really big. Believing this, for a time I went fishing with a hook that would make Moby Dick break into a sweat. I still caught no big fish.

At about five in the morning, just as the sun was about to rise over the hills, the line in my hand went taut and hard as fencing wire. The pull of the line toward the water was so strong that the nylon started to slip between my fingers. I could hardly believe it. As I followed the line into the water, I could see it darting and circling about the surface as if I had hooked a mad shark. My heart pounded and leaped into my throat as if I were riding the Big Dipper at Luna Park. All I could think was, My God, it must be a bloody whale. What if I lose it? What if I lose it? Please don't let me lose it.

Gradually and slowly I wound my line around its plastic reel. Bit by bit, I could feel the fish come slowly closer to the surface. Soon I would see it as long as its frenzied behavior didn't wrap my line around the bollards of the pier. Oh I hope it doesn't wrap itself around the bollards of the bloody pier. Please not the bollards. At least let me get a glimpse of the monster for my birthday, I thought to myself. Finally, I could see the fish. It was a silver bream, maybe two pounds in weight.

It swam this way and that so that I could see its beautiful scales and size in the infant morning light. In an instant it was flapping about in the air with my heart flapping with it and then—*bang*— there it was on the deck of the pier with me. Two pounds at least, I swear, not an ounce less. Could have been more. I quickly disgorged the hook and put the fish in my flour bag, which I had brought with me for more modest game. I sat there euphoric. What a fish! What a catch! What incredible luck! Happy birthday, you lucky mug! You just caught the biggest bloody fish in the wooorld!

I know what joy is. I was a thrilled-neck lizard then. I was as stoked as any surfy after riding a great wave. I packed up my gear and left immediately. Fishing any more that morning felt like being greedy or ungrateful or both. A man even tried to buy my fish from me in the train on the way home. Imagine, an offer to buy my happiness. Had any offers like *that* lately?

In the busyness and banality of everyday life, our emotions and experiences sometimes assume a quality of sameness. Some events can also get us down. If there are no peak experiences, no joy to be found, year in and year out, what will balance that "sinking" feeling? Forget about your daily milk or fiber intake. Are you getting enough joy?

# 11

# God

૱ᎦᏟᏒ

In my work, the topic of God pops up nearly every week. Someone who was dying of cancer once asked me why God let the cancer develop in her—she was thirty years old and had two small children.

A colleague once said that when she was told that Christ was the center of all artistic expression, she immediately understood what it meant.

I wish I did.

On another occasion, I received a small note and a photograph in the mail from a woman who had read a piece I had written on death. The photograph portrayed her collie-like dog standing on all fours in the center of her backyard. She wrote that her *previous* dog, now dead, appeared in the top right-hand corner of the photograph. This picture, she said, was a "gift from God."

I stared at the white squiggle marks in the top right-hand corner of the photograph, but confess I could not see another dog.

Perhaps the white squiggles resembled a terrier face and two paws, but it looked to me as if her dog had become a cartoon character in the afterlife. Maybe I was looking in the wrong place. I do not disbelieve that her phantom dog was there. I didn't know what to think.

I don't understand what type of God does this to people's photos. I don't know why God would do this to a photo and not turn around and stop my thirty-year-old acquaintance from being taken away from her children. I feel that the idea of God *could* be a good one. But if God is a fact, I am uncertain whether we have met. At least that's how it feels a lot of the time.

If I were convinced of God's existence, it would not solve the other problem that seems to be joined at the hip. What does God do for a living, for example? God doesn't stop wars, cancers, kidnaping and murder. God doesn't punish drivers who change lanes without indicating, or those who use mobile phones while wandering all over the road. God doesn't protect anyone, or, if God does, there seems to be no regular system or pattern or plan that is easily discernible. And that's only a modest list.

Some people, like the person who sent me the dog photo, tell me that they can "see" God. Perhaps not the face of God, but God's handiwork, God's way, God's will, or God's grace and support. This *may* be true.

For a long time I was no good at all at visual puzzles. These were large, multicolored pictures of repetitive patterns. You were instructed to stare at the picture for a time so that eventually a three-dimensional picture would emerge from the seemingly random chaos of the picture, assuming that you were looking at it "the right way."

On and off for about a year, I could never master this skill. That was about ten years ago. Now I only have to look at those puzzles for about fifteen seconds and I can "see." I have now "learnt" how to "see" the picture beneath the picture.

Maybe God's influence is like this. Maybe I will take most of my life to "see" God's will, support or grace.

There have been moments in my life—solitary moments—when I felt something, or someone, physically near me, but I could see no one. There were several times as a young boy when, in a dark church, I was lighting a candle and felt something like company. When I looked around me, there was nobody to be seen.

Another time, on a beach, I observed a sunrise alone and had the same experience.

Once, in the middle of a serious car accident, as the car tumbled and rolled around like paper in a wild breeze, that feeling of company drew attention to itself once again.

What was it I felt? And did any of it "help" me?

Perhaps in church, on the beach, and in the car, I was experiencing "depersonalization." This happens when the intellect and the emotions temporarily part ways and gaze dispassionately at each other. It occurs a lot in crises, but it can also happen in sleep-like, drug-induced, and altered mental states. It can be a protective mechanism of the brain under stress or threat. So, the company I felt could have been my own.

But why do I need to be protected against sunrises and candle-lit churches, I have to ask? Where are the stress and trauma in them?

So it seems to come to this. If God is a feeling—a brain or religious one—God might be there when you are alone. And this might be because, whatever the Grand Plan of life is, there is a basic recognition—a minimal agreement by the brain, or by God, that life is tough enough as it is without being alone. If you care to notice, God or the brain will always be there to put an arm around your shoulders. The candle warms inside me, as the sunrise does and, when I crash sometimes there is a strange sensation of someone holding my hand.

Maybe the meaning of God is presence. And perhaps companionship is what God or the brain does for a living. In a tough and uncertain life, the distinction may not be important. It is not clear that the influence of one necessarily dispenses with the other. But it is good to know that sometimes you can be alone but not abandoned, because behind the repetitive buzz of everyday life there may be a deeper picture of companionship. Some puzzles might take longer to see.

# 12

# Your Best Offer

ഔഃ

Most of us like to think that when we die we will have left earth a little better for our having lived here. We hope that we have made a difference. In many accounts of near-death experiences, people report meeting a bright being of light. This being initiates a life review for the dying or dead person by asking them a question, something like, What have you done with your life? Or, What have you to show me? (with the same underlying meaning).

The writer Robert Fulghum tells the story of a no-hoper who was a failure in every job he held. Although he came from a well-to-do family, John Pierpont attempted careers in teaching, law, business, poetry, religious ministry, and politics, but was no good at any of them. He died as a government clerk in the treasury department and was no star there either. His life was singularly unremarkable. But he did have an endearing habit of dreaming up musical ditties for children at Christmas time. All of us owe a great debt to him for the legacy of "Jingle Bells," one of the simplest and most charming Christmas songs.

I was moved by Fulghum's story, but it prompted me to ask myself if my legacy could be anything like that of John Pierpont? I sing the first few words of most carols loudly and then hum the rest until the chorus, when I can remember more of the words. This is not the most fertile ground for a career in song writing. And I know I am not alone, not only in composing, but also in the matter of personal legacy. It would be wonderful to have contributed to and be known for something as charming as "Jingle Bells," but I do not think it will be my destiny.

I watched the 1946 Fred Capra film called *It's a Wonderful Life* to see his view of how an ordinary person—like you or me—might leave an important legacy. The film follows George Bailey (played to perfection by Jimmy Stewart), a small-town banker who is forced to follow in his father's footsteps as a money lender, forgoing a much longed-for college education, overseas trips, and the chance to widen his creative and professional horizons. A crisis sees George on the brink of suicide. And then he is visited by an angel in the form of a wise old man.

This man shows George how life would have turned out for others if he had not been doing his job as a kind person and banker. We are taken on a Dickensian tour of George's past life and experiences, which shows us what they would be like *without* him. What a difference! George's life had touched hundreds of others. Even his small acts had telescoped into enormous outcomes for other people.

We do our best, when we can, to be helpful. And we hope that when the sums are done by someone—even ourselves—that the good we do might outweigh the good that we fail to do. Everyone leaves a legacy. Even small babies.

Near my university is a large suburban cemetery. Against one border lies a long strip of empty land punctuated by large, old pine trees. For many years, a large local hospital buried stillborn babies and others here who had died within minutes of their birth.

Since the 1950s, the hospital had buried more than five hundred such little babies. From about the early 1980s, the women who gave birth to them made a steady pilgrimage from the hospital to this unmarked place in the local cemetery. A quarter of a century did not dim the memory of that intimate relationship between a mother and the small life she carried.

A steady number of small plaques have appeared since the 1990s around the shaded areas beneath the pine trees, and every year their number silently grows. Even little lives leave a legacy, however short and sad that life may have been. Ultimately, this is a legacy of attachment, of love.

The Chinese have an instructive story about the minutiae of everyday life. In the seventeenth century, a very holy Buddhist nun set out to collect subscriptions to cast a new statue of the Buddha. Positioning herself at the intersection of a large road, she was approached by an amiable madman. On hearing her mission, the man remarked that generosity was one of his better personal qualities and promptly handed over two coins, the equivalent of a fraction of a farthing. He then wrote his name in large letters in the subscription book.

In the course of time, the nun returned with her subscriptions, and the work of smelting the copper for casting the statue began. But despite increasing the fuel to the furnace, the copper failed to melt in any substantial way. Nothing the workmen did seemed to help, until finally the foreman of the plant observed that an offering of great value must have been missing.

The workers and the foreman went to the nun to check the subscription book and found that only two coins—those from the madman had been kept from the smelting. The nun had withheld them because they were so small. Reflecting that the madman's donation may have been of the highest value, the nun threw the coins into the cauldron, allowing the metal to melt into fluid and the casting to begin.

Perhaps the Greek legend of carrying coins for the boatman to take you across the river Styx is less relevant as a message for life than the Chinese legend of the madman's gift. Small lives or little carols; bankers and madmen; little coins all, and all treasured and important. What coins do you bring for the nun who waits at the intersection?

# 13

# Monsters

ℰᏖᏟᎡ

In the Melanesian islands of New Hebrides, a young man must undergo a remarkable test to ascertain whether he is worthy of life. This rite of passage imitates the path of the soul on its final journey to the land of the dead. The symbolic rite initiates the young man into life.

The initiate walks to a cave. At the entrance, the symbolic meeting place of life and death, a devouring female ghost sits blocking his way. Her name is Le-Hev-Hev. With her finger, this monster draws a geometric figure in the sand and waits patiently to be approached. At first, the sight of her makes the man confused by his own fear. But he regains his senses and moves towards her. As he does so, Le-Hev-Hev rubs out half of the design. Now the initiate, who is also known as the "dead man," must redraw the figure or be destroyed by Le-Hev-Hev.

In the New Hebrides, this complex and mysterious geometric figure is translated as "The Path" or "The Way."

The Melanesian test is a wonderful symbol of the cultural and existential tests that life frequently throws before us. We each walk our own way in life and during that time we make important plans for our future. These may not be grand plans, but they are life-expectant patterns.

An essential part of our design requires that we be present. When we see trouble up ahead, it can be disorienting. Serious problems in marriage or work, for example, can prompt a crisis in confidence. The prospect of death and serious illness can propel us into facing those uncertainties with even greater doubt, and these may easily and quickly drive us to despair and anxiety and to ideas of early surrender.

All of these can lead us to feel that we are losing our way, even surrendering the will to live, tempting us to withdraw from the challenge that faces us. And that venture, like the monster Le-Hev-Hev, can be intimidating. Sometimes gradually, and at other times quite quickly, we look at the pattern of the life before us and realize that someone or something has rubbed half the pattern away.

Now the question is: can we redraw it?

There are several clues that you need before you answer. You must see how much of the pattern remains. This pattern is complex, but the complexity is good. The patterns that remain are your past life. And they are there because Le-Hev-Hev cannot erase them. Your past experiences and meanings are irrevocably yours. Only possibilities can be tampered with.

The famous Viennese psychoanalyst Victor Frankl argued that the trick in life is to capture as much potential as possible and turn it into actualities, your stored treasure of the present and past. Then, no one and no thing can take it away from you.

In a way, the missing pattern in the sand might be extended and drawn by attempting to make it mirror or reflect the existing pattern. Many attempt to draw their future in this way, especially those who are happy with their past life. But the missing pattern might be redrawn differently from the one on the other side, especially by those wishing to forge a new life pattern.

But ask yourself this: does Le-Hev-Hev really care what you scrawl in the sand? Is the test an artistic one? Is life a matter of graphic design?

The message of the Melanesian initiation legend is surely not a test of memory or art, but the challenge of facing Le-Hev-Hev—of facing your monsters, your worst fears.

I always remember the joke about the man falling from the top of a skyscraper. Office workers inside could hear him mutter words as he was seen passing each floor. Someone phoned friends several floors below to encourage them to listen carefully to the words as the falling man passed their floor. As the man passed their floor, he was heard to exclaim: "So far so good."

The ground coming up fast for the falling man is no less intimidating than Le-Hev-Hev, and the image for both is death. But a certain level of detachment—the mental concentration of a very difficult effort, or a life-affirming sense of humor—enables us to draw the missing pattern without talking ourselves into early submission. As you sweat it out with Le-Hev-Hev, remember that she is only in this game because, unlike you, she hasn't got a life. You have. Hang on to it right to the end.

# 14

# Astronaut

ഇ‍ദ‍ൿ

In the world of astrophysical theory, there is a lot of speculation about space and time travel. If we were to think about distances in space in terms of conventional rocket travel, for example, interstellar journeys would take forever. That's why science fiction films always invent technologies like "jump gates" or "warp drives" or speak in terms of "light speed." Some writers expound even stranger theories about "worm-holes," for example. These are odd places in the universe, where normal concepts of space and time do not apply. Entering those worm-holes would enable a traveler to cover distances in time previous thought inconceivable.

All of this is speculation, of course. Eventually, however, we will need to resolve the problem of vast distances if, as human beings, we are to have a serious attempt at space travel. Running to the comer store is one thing but, if you want to go from Sydney to Perth in under a week, you'll need to come up with something better than running shoes. The world of the spirit has similar challenges. And if you think "worm-holes" are a weird idea for space travel, take another look at Christmas tinsel and mind-travel. Yes, Christmas tinsel.

I was doing my food shopping the other day, and although it was October, the supermarket had a little corner selling Christmas tinsel for the early birds among us. I stopped to look at this tinsel, I mean, *really* looked at it. There were red and gold garlands like loops of Hawaiian leis, and little green and red tinsel-colored Santas; there were blue and silver tinsel stars; and red and white barber-shop candy walking-sticks. When I stopped to look carefully, it only took a few seconds to be transported back to a time when all these were not toys or tree decorations but objects from another world.

Tinsel, when you think about it, is a highly unusual material. For a child, it has unusual properties. When you grow up, a lingering look at that tinsel can have an equally unusual effect.

As I stared at the tinsel, I remembered the first time that I saw a tree covered in it. I was very young, perhaps four or five years old. The tree looked to me to be about twelve or fifteen feet high. (I'm sure it was only half that size really, but I was very short then.) The tree towered over me, and the tinsel looked as if all of it was emanating from a single point in the ceiling—probably a large hairy starfish-like object at the top of the tree. At the bottom, were Christmas presents. There were many multi-colored boxes, all with little tickets attached— gift cards with blue writing and pictures of reindeer faces or barber-shop candy sticks. Some were tinsel-colored, with ribbons, and some were wrapped in green and red paper, with pictures of snow scenes, stars, or Santa faces on them. Pine cones were spread around among the gifts. The tree smelt like a forest and there was "Santa snow" on some of the branches— a white spray put on some of the branches which, I discovered later, came out of a can. Now, I ask you, is there anything ordinary about this scene?

When you read the words on this page, do you remember your first impressions of tinsel and Christmas? Christmas is an unusual time, isn't it? Even if you regard this as only a children's time, you would have to say that the physical decorations—the pine tree, the garish metallic colors, the visual emphasis on kindly faces, reindeer, stars, or pudding, the pleasant smelling reminders of forests, dinners, or night-time reunions—are absorbing, hypnotizing, and distracting for their distinctiveness and their formal associations and messages.

For a moment you stop; you become someone else; you are diverted; your soul and mind have left the building. You are traveling, only you know where.

As I look up from the supermarket tinsel, other shoppers are staring at me. My partner has finished the shopping, and she is queuing at the check-out casting an impatient look my way. I do not know how long I have been standing there, but clearly other shoppers think I have escaped some minders. And my partner thinks I have been shirking my responsibilities to the weekly household grazing needs. But in these moments I have traveled from my self with the aid of a spiritual "warp drive," "jump gate," or "worm-hole." How important is this technology?

When people talk about some of their fears or their physical suffering—their pain, breathlessness, or other discomforts—problems that do not easily go away—we talk about the need for a self-administered technology for spiritual and physical pain, a kind of ejection seat for the self. People try mental imaging techniques, relaxation and breathing exercises, or meditation. All of these are good. I once took up tai chi and found that this was great for stress control. It gave me great peace and time-out from my "busy brain." I later discovered that golf had the same effect on me.

What I found difficult about tai chi, though, and what many people with life-threatening illness also tell me is that getting into the calming image is difficult for them. "Emptying their minds" of thought is very hard.

If this is your problem too, do I have a jump-gate for you. Try holding a handful of Christmas tinsel in your hand. Play an old song you love. Hold a favorite bracelet to your chest. Take an old photo from the family album. Look at that old postcard from Rio. Look or listen carefully. Give yourself to these pieces. Look kindly at them. The first memory will soon come to you, and then the next and, then, you will have joined me in the supermarket. You have become a space-traveler of the human spirit.

# 15

# Planning and Preparing

❧❧

These days my dear old mother lives alone in a small apartment block of six units mainly occupied by elderly people. The exception was an apartment rented by Larry, a single man in his fifties living on an invalid pension. Larry had an advanced cancer and made weekly visits to the hospital for treatments. He had heard my mother say that I worked in palliative care and he asked her if I could drop by at his apartment when next I visited her. He was keen to meet someone who "knew about cancer and things" and would dearly love to have a few minutes to talk to me.

I arrived at Mum's apartment only to be quickly ushered across to Larry's place with whispered exhortations to "help the poor man." I knocked on Larry's door as instructed and was welcomed by the friendly and solicitous chatter and mirth of my mother's neighbor. Larry looked well, his recent weight loss making him appear much younger than his fifty-something years. As we chatted about this and that, I noticed that the lounge room was lined with removalists boxes. The only furniture I could see was the chair I happened to be sitting on (Larry sat on a removalists' box), and a small radio and stereo system. I inquired casually if Larry was moving, adding that my mother was not aware of his plans. Larry looked puzzled and said: "I'm not moving Allan. I'm dying."

"Well, we're all dying aren't we?" I said.

"No, seriously Allan, the doctors tell me that I'm not long for this world. I'm just making preparations, that's all."

"I understand that, Larry, but this isn't preparing to die, is it? This is planning for it."

"Well, what's the difference?" Larry said.

And so we reflected together about the differences.

Death only takes a few minutes, sometimes even less. It's a small event with some significant administrative consequences. What to do with your furniture and belongings? What to do with your remaining money? Are any survivors of your family taken care of personally and materially?

Life, on the other hand, is a big project. What to eat every day? How will I cope with the social challenges at home or work? How will I defuse my daily stresses and refresh my daily dreams and hopes? How can I be a friend or cope with disappointment? What must I do this minute or this hour, in the long and uncertain challenge of manufacturing meaning out of my everyday tasks?

In these ways, you plan a holiday and prepare for the trip; plan a wedding but prepare the menus; plan a party but prepare the invitations; plan a garden but prepare the soil; plan a meal but prepare the food; plan for success but prepare for emergencies.

We always plan for the Big Picture. Life is the Big Picture and an important part of the planning for it must be to prepare for death, always a certainty in life, however small and brief the actual event. Death itself is the small thing here. Life is the big one, right? How realistic is it to plan to live when you are facing death? Ask yourself this—who is the exception?

Remember, to employ an old pirate's analogy, we all walk the plank. It's just that some of us do so with a blindfold and some of us without. The most common problem these days appears to be that those with the blindfold rarely prepare for their drop and those who prepare for their drop stop enjoying the walk. Dare to ignore the critics. Do two things at once. And remember—don't stop enjoying the walk.

# 16

# A Living Thing

ॐ

From the cradle to the grave it's hard to do your own thing. When I was at school, my heart and mind were at home among the flowers, vegetables, and animals I had there. Sometimes during my lessons I would work busily drawing pictures of them. As I grew older I became interested in rock 'n' roll. I took up the bass guitar and played in a band. During school hours I would write out song lyrics or music for pieces that I might play on the weekend or after school. My school marks reflected this lack of dedication. I was always near to or at the bottom of my class.

One day, in senior school, the principal asked me what my school leaving plans were. I replied that I wanted to go to university. He remarked dryly that the closest I was likely to get to a university was "painting the front fence." But I *did* go to university.

I studied for an Arts degree and then, attracted to topics such as death and dying, decided to go on to medical school. I lasted two years in the medical faculty—two of the most unhappy years of my life. I found the rote-learning tradition of study soul-destroying and the company little better.

People thought I was crazy even to consider leaving medicine. I was throwing one of life's great opportunities away, they said. But I was after bigger game, the pursuit of something that would capture my heart and soul, some greater and more satisfying meaning for my life. I became unemployed for a year, applying for forty jobs unsuccessfully. I finally managed to secure a one-year teaching contract with a small rural college. Some friends thought I had fallen on hard times, but it didn't seem that way to me. I was simply searching for my own personal meaning, eventually discovering a need to return to university to read for a Ph.D.

Of all the possible things to study, I chose the topic of dying, and I chose it with a strengthened and renewed commitment. Friends warned that I would find it difficult to get a job with a doctorate on that topic, but I did get one. I worked in several academic departments where my work on death and dying was viewed as eccentric. In the academic world, the attainment of a full professorship often depends on how "mainstream" your work is viewed and how much grant money you can attract for it. I had obtained little grant money. Few governments want to fund books and research into near-death experiences, social aspects of dying, spirituality, or the meaning of death. But eventually I *did* become a full professor.

I am grateful for my successes, even more so because neither I nor many others near to me thought that any should be expected. But along the way all I have ever wanted to do is what I wanted to do. I neither sought praise nor invited the criticism I have endured.

And so it is with these experiences that I reflect on the consequences of not conforming, or to put a more positive spin on it, of following my heart's desire. Even now, I think of life as a series of sticky steps, each attempting to grab and hold your foot to its place, preventing it from moving to the next. You can hear the sucking sounds as you attempt to pull your foot up to make the next step: why leave here when you have it so good; you don't have the experience, ability or the networks for that goal; you shouldn't gamble with a good thing; you don't have what it takes; look before you leap; it might not work out; you might be making a big mistake. And frankly, it's all true.

Failures, mistakes, inability, inexperience, fallibility and vulnerability happen and, then, with time, experience, courage, determination, imagination, support, quick thinking, and just plain luck, you can gradually transform them—and shock a good-sized audience into the bargain!

What do people tell me now? They say I'm lucky, a one-off, a fluke. There is only room for one of me. The lyrics change, but the skeptics sing them to the same old tune. As I say to people who live with a life-threatening illness, it is not what is "best" for you or "best" for them, whoever "they" are, it's what you *want* to do that is most important. The world of human affairs is full of people who will offer you reasons for not doing things. It will always be your voice against a million but remember this: the clock is ticking.

Enroll in that ballroom-dancing class; connect to the Internet *now*; buy that boat; stand for that position; apply for that job; join that experiment; visit that healer; go on that trip; make that phone call; embrace that passion you have deep in your heart. Ignore that doubter on your left, and that nay-sayer on your right. The wind may blow or the rain may fall, but neither should deter a bird from flying. There is plenty of time to play dead. For now, while there is breath in you, be a living thing.

# 17

# Shareholders

৯৩

Despite the deadly association that cancer evokes in most people's minds, it has been estimated that the number of people who experience a spontaneous remission of their cancer—an inexplicable disappearance of the disease—is about one person in every 100,000 people. They are pretty good odds, I feel. At least they are better odds than winning lotto, and with lotto, it's only money, right? It's not your life.

When I say this to people, they often respond that these are bad odds. People don't often feel lucky; they don't feel special. But think about how often you are surprised.

There was a time in my life, between the ages of twelve and fifteen, when every boy in my suburb had a bike. Mum couldn't afford to buy me one, so joining my friends in this graduation to this new form of transportation was out of the question. Day in and day out I would leave school through the side door of my house, walk along the long veranda, drop down the small set of steps into the side garden and leave by the side gate next to our privet hedges. From there I would run down several streets to get to the station and catch the train to school.

One day, when I arrived by the gate at the privet hedges, there, half buried in that privet, was an old black bicycle with flat tires. I couldn't believe it! Who would? What are the odds of this happening? Of all the houses that someone might choose to dump an old bicycle, they chose mine! Understandably, since that day, privet hedges hold a special place in my heart.

A couple of years after this incident, my mother agreed to send me to Tasmania on a school excursion. This was an expensive school function, and there would be no spending money for me except for anything I might save between now and then. My pocket money was so hand-to-mouth that saving much seemed unlikely, a dark fate for a compulsive souvenir collector. One day as I was walking along a rail line looking for bottles to collect so that I could return them for their refunds, I looked across at a small pile of dirt. There, like the last slice of cake on a plate, was a twenty-dollar note. Now, I ask you, it may not be unusual to find some coins by a railway line, but notes? What are the chances of finding a twenty-dollar bill sitting in the open? Is the wind so fussy that it chooses only to blow newspapers around but leaves money for scavenging kids? In those days (the 1960s), twenty dollars was a small fortune. Not only could I look forward to buying a plastic Tasmanian devil or a snowball of Hobart, I could now almost become a shareholder in the factory that made them.

At those times I felt touched by what religious people have called a blessing—the idea that something more powerful and superior has bestowed on you a happy favor. I felt grateful but had no idea to whom I should feel that gratitude. Who had bestowed this great fortune on me? Maybe it was God. Maybe it was sheer luck. Maybe it was physical chaos in the universe downloading yet another coincidence. Pretty lousy explanations, I admit, but these things keep happening. Uncertainties, coincidences, luck (good and bad), surprises and shocks, flukes and oddities happen every day. They occur at work and at home, and in love and politics. They bedevil your search for car keys, your application for a job, your odd perfect record of avoiding colds or of getting them. Even when traveling to foreign countries, as unlikely as it seems, you often bump into someone you know. It seems to me that the odd thing about anyone winning the lotto is not that someone wins—people do win—but that more people aren't winning all the time. Rather than predictable cycles of events, it is diversity and randomness which seem, well, the *real norm*.

And if you stop, think and carefully take the time to recall all your coincidences, surprises and flukes in your every day life, you will quickly warm to the idea that a 100,000 to 1 set of odds is not bad at all. The trick is not to become obsessed, with a possibility, in other words, to avoid treating a possibility as something you can control. Disappointment ties down that road. Ask any gambling addict.

As you can see, possibility and uncertainty, are the good and loyal friends of optimism. And optimism, when it has these two friends, not only puts you into possession of the odd blessing or two, but gives you enough to be a shareholder in the factory.

# 18

# Your Fortune in Cairo

## ഇൻ

I met a woman some years ago who, on discovering that she had a serious, spreading cancer, began to visit all the places where she had previously lived. These included the towns and suburbs and the houses and flats of her childhood. She would make her way to those spots and sit in her car or at a place across the road and reflect on her memories of them. I asked her what she meant by this pilgrimage to past places. Some of her motivation, she said, lay in symbolically farewelling parts of her life. But another side of it was the inner contemplation she derived from each trip she made. She could not say, or perhaps would not say, exactly what these thoughts were.

I had come across this experience before but in connection with other journeys. Several people discussed their choice of decision to visit a healing place, often feeling no need to disclose this to their doctors. I asked them why they felt the need to visit healing places such as Fatima or Lourdes, and why they did not discuss their plans with their doctors. Unlike other people, who were traveling with a clear idea about their aspirations for a cure, many of these people were not clear about why they paid visits to healing places. They were adamant, however, that these pilgrimages helped them in some way deep inside, gave them some kind of comfort and hope. They would say that they saw their doctors as people concerned with practical outcomes rather than the less tangible but no less important issues of inner meaning at a time of personal crisis.

So what did they gain from their pilgrimages to past or "sacred" places? What did they, and perhaps we, hope to gain by making these kinds of journeys?

There is another tale from the Arabian Nights that tells of a man in Baghdad who had a wonderful dream. In it, a man appeared before him and declared: "Your fortune lies in Cairo. Go and seek it there."

The next morning, the dreamer set out on his journey to Cairo. It was a long and hard trip and, after a few weeks, he arrived in Cairo just as evening fell. Knowing no one, the dreamer found a sheltered spot in the courtyard of a mosque. During the night a band of robbers broke in, making a lot of noise in the process. The police arrived, but it was too late. Instead of the robbers, the police found the dreamer who they beat up severely. They took him to prison where he waited for three days before being summonsed by the chief of police.

"What were you doing in the mosque?" asked the chief.

The dreamer told the police chief about his dream and his journey to Cairo.

The police chief looked pityingly at the poor dreamer and said that he too had similar dreams. Indeed, he had one dream three times in which a man had come to him and told him to go to Baghdad. That there in a particular cobbled street, lined by a certain type of palm tree he would find a house with certain kinds of courtyards, steps and a fountain. Under the fountain he would find a fortune.

But, as the police chief pointed out wisely, if he had followed his dreams he would have been wandering permanently. He gave the dreamer a small sum of money and advised him to return home immediately.

On hearing this story, the dreamer recognized his own house in the description of the police chief's story. He gratefully accepted the money and hurried home straight to the fountain and uncovered the hidden fortune predicted in the police chief's dream.

The words in his dream were true: he *did* find his fortune in Cairo but not in the form he imagined and not without great trials. In the end, the actual fortune was in his own backyard, in the back reaches of his own self

Paradoxically, sometimes you need to go out to go in. You may need the motion of a journey, the strangeness of a new place, or the caress of old familiar places to begin and nurture a new journey of self-discovery. Just thinking about a problem may not help. Long dwelling on the meaning of your life in all your usual places may not help you uncover the personal meanings that *are* in you but require some special jolt or experience to uncover.

There is a place inside me that I call home. But it is not always easy for me to make my way there. When I am troubled and the darkness of those troubles clouds my thoughts and confuses my feelings, I can lose my way.

At these times—which may be brought on by worry, tiredness or sorrow—we need a symbolic light within ourselves to find the way home. Maybe sacred places, and sometimes sacred faces, help light the way for us at these times.

Cairo did not yield a fortune for the dreamer, but it did reveal the secret of its location. And for many of us, the secret of that location is the very thing we need. Sometimes, you need to seek your fortune in Cairo.

# 19

# What will it be like
# for you?

ಹಿಂದೆ

People ask me if I know what it is like to die. I have a colleague, a cancer and palliative care specialist, who always answers that question by saying that he hasn't the wildest idea. No one has come back to tell him. I feel differently about this question.

I believe that there are people who have felt that they have had an encounter with death and lived to tell the tale. The problem for me is that I am not one of them. This means that I do not know their story from the inside. I can read about the jubilation on hearing the announcement of the end of the Second World War, but I don't really know how that felt for people at the time. Their story is not my story. Reading about an experience does not hand me that experience. Instead, I am given insight, that is, some clue to that experience.

Being present when someone dies does not reveal their experience to you either. You stand there as a carer or a bystander.

You respond to their death as a survivor. Working with corpses day in and day out in autopsy or in the city morgue does not acquaint you with *death*. Your knowledge of human anatomy increases, certainly. And you begin to understand bodily trauma and failure, disease and putrefaction in a close-up, intimate way. But the meaning of death is nowhere to be found. The experience and meaning of *dying* has long fled these settings and environments.

If we cannot be present during dying and understand, if we cannot read about dying and understand, if we cannot examine the remains of the dying and understand, are we condemned to being ignorant about what dying is like? Is there no compromise between ignorance and the real thing? I think the solution to our problem of understanding dying is like so much else in life—we must stop looking elsewhere for *our* meanings. In the end, we must take what basic clues we can from the reading and the verbal testimony of those who have gone before us.

All of this must then be tempered and forged with the knowledge of what kind of person you think you are. Want to know what it's like being you? Well, don't look for examples from other people. Use your own experiences to tell you about you. Climb down from the abstract heights of other people's stories and come back to earth and occupy your own shoes.

Ah,

well then,

What is it like to die?

How do you like surprises?

What is it like to "go to sleep?"

What is it like to leave on a long trip?

Have you ever been suddenly out of work?

How do you react and cope with uncertainty, doubt, or fear?

Do you like mysteries, and how do you feel about solving them?

Have you ever been forced to give up someone that you really loved?

How do you feel about good-byes that may be forever, or for a long time?

What is it like to enter an unknown room, not knowing if it is full or empty?

Faced with limited resources, how good are you at "making the best of it?"

How do you react to being seriously ill, to nausea, pain, immobility and to unpredictable cycles of all these and more?

Well?

Don't just rush through these questions. Go back and take a few minutes to think about each one and answer them honestly. Some answers will require great personal effort. They need some working at. The answers to these questions will probably give you your best clues to what dying will be like for you. If you are honestly interested in that answer, you must, with equal truth, search among your answers to these questions. And what of the actual minute of death itself?

It is surprising the number of people who report experiences when they are unconscious—meeting old friends or relatives long thought very dead. Equally enlightening is the number of people who seem to see, or who claim to see, some of these dead friends come to collect them on their deathbed just minutes or even seconds before their actual death. These are old, even ancient experiences that have been reported for centuries in diverse cultures. Maybe they tell us that, at best, death may be reunion and new life. At the very least, death may hold some small fragment of comforting experience near the end itself.

Death, as a personal journey, may hold out a future for you. But the final answer (worse luck!) only reveals itself when it is your turn to go.

The Australian poet Les Murray sent a positive but rather glib message to a dying friend expressing the hope that his mate might have "an easy death, with surprises at the end."

I will go one further in the well-wishers' stakes. For all the trouble that dying can be, any surprises that come along at the end had better be worth it, don't you think? Let's hope the surprises are good ones.

# 20

# Everlasting Things

୫୬୯୫

I am in Hong Kong Harbor in 1960. The air is perfumed and the sky is warm and blue. The harbor is absolutely gorgeous. I am riding the Star Ferry across to Kowloon, and the sails of a thousand junks leap toward the sky like tigers. All around me are junks, so many that I can't count them all. Some sail alone; others are strung together like so many crest-shaped beads. Inside and on top of them, mothers cry out to their children; others stand silently looking at a pot or some other object on the deck. Some look at me as the ferry heaves and rocks past them in a noisy whiff of engine oil and sea spray.

In my heart and mind, this is an eternal scene, an everlasting thing for me, even now, despite the fact that the junks, and the poor of those times, are all gone.

When I resurrect this memory, it is like so many others because, like other moments of importance to me, this one comes with temperature, smells, feelings, thoughts, and a million colors. Memories, it was once said, are given to us so that we may smell the roses in winter.

This was also Arthur Mee's view. Arthur Mee was a children's book editor in England at the turn of the twentieth century. Arthur was no ordinary editor of children's stories. He wrote and edited few "stories for children," and the joke went that as many adults read Arthur's books as the children for which they were ostensibly bought. Some of the titles of his books suggest matters above and beyond simply playful ideas: *Arthur Mee's Golden Year; Arthur Mee's Wonderful Day; One Thousand Beautiful Things;* and the very wonderful *Arthur Mee's Book of Everlasting Things.* And what do we find inside the covers of this last book?

Inside *The Book of Everlasting Things* we find essays by Milton, Abe Lincoln, Plato, Ruskin, Macaulay, or Thomas More; we find photographs of artworks by van Dyke, Filippino Lippi, or Michelangelo. There are photos of Nefertiti—Queen of Egypt— and sculpture by Rodin or Donatello. Other pages show us French ivory carvings from the fifteenth century or Greek vases from the museum in Athens. Mee reproduces poems from Keats, Shelley, Browning, Byron, Cowper and Tennyson, and many more. Sections of the Bible are reproduced, excerpts from the stories of Edgar Allan Poe, passages from Robinson Crusoe, even letters from Cromwell or Charlotte Bronte. *The Book of Everlasting Things* contains 352 pages of snippets from great writing and art. But there is more to Arthur's books than diversity and divers charms.

One of his books contains antiwar messages to children, describing the case of a First World War soldier, a young man who died slowly of his injuries. Imagine antiwar stories in the 1920s—and directed at children! Arthur Mee employed the metaphor of the day or the year to signify the cycle from birth to death. *The Book of Everlasting Things* deals directly with the problem of death itself. Without doubt, Arthur Mee was a man before his time. What did this unusual man have to say about the subject of death?

Arthur's idea of death was intrinsically linked to his view of "everlasting things." He felt that they were invisible and included great ideas of invention but also beauty, wisdom, love, dreams, and what Arthur called "the spirit of God." All could be momentarily glimpsed in art and poetry and the grandeur of physical scenery. I say "momentarily glimpsed" because Arthur argued that all visible things were subject to passing away. Poems could burn, physical bodies deteriorate, and cathedrals fall, but love and wisdom, and the dreams generated by them, ensured their everlasting survival in other forms and sites. Everlasting things were matters of the spirit rather than physical substance, things of meaning rather than physical vessels that carried or prompted those meanings.

Are you and I everlasting things? Contemporary science writers argue that nothing is destroyed in the universe. Matter simply changes from one form into another. Arthur Mee would see this as low-brow survival. It would matter little to Mee whether a part of his brain that enabled him to remember Kent is now helping to create a new solar system somewhere in the universe. It is difficult to get excited or inspired about the survival of one's atoms.

Arthur Mee believed in God and the survival of personality beyond death. In this context, everlasting things were linked to the divine spirit in humanity. He belonged to a time when it was perhaps easier to believe in the divine spirit. Today many of us are not so sure. If our atoms survive us, well, good luck to them. But most of us don't care a toss for our atoms any more than for the bunions on our feet. What really matters are our friends, family and lovers; the striving to be of value and of service to others, however modestly; the treasury of our cherished memories and dreams. These underpin our character and our hopes just as they give us our sense of identity and continuity. These are the things which most of us would wish were everlasting.

I cherish my memories of Hong Kong and want to visit Hong Kong in 1960 whenever I choose—my brain atoms can go hang.

But is the pleasure of my Hong Kong memory in the actual memory of Hong Kong, pure and simple? Or is the suppression of other things when I am inside that memory a hidden part of the pleasure? Forgetting my troubles, or my home, temporarily allows me to focus fully and solely on my Hong Kong experience. Isn't that forgetting also an important part of good holidays or weekends?

What, then, is the real source of the pleasure—the remembering or the forgetting? Obviously a little of both.

The mythical adventurer Odysseus came upon a race of people called the Lotus Eaters in his travels. He found that when you ate the lotus plants that grew there, you completely forgot your home and became attached to the land of the Lotus Eaters. Some of Odysseus's sailors who had eaten these plants had to be restrained on his ship if they were to return home. They were besotted with staying in what they had forgotten was a foreign land, a place that was not their home.

I sometimes wonder if we are the original Lotus Eaters in this life of ours. We forget while we are here and remember when, after a struggle against final repatriation, we return home. In a reverse use of this analogy, materialist thinkers believe we do all our remembering here and all our forgetting at death. In either case, perhaps forgetting and remembering are essential to the bringing together of the different dimensions of personal development and fulfillment. These qualities are essential to performing our tasks here and now in this life—as limited creatures of the flesh or as spiritual beings. Forgetting and remembering are inseparable. Like life and death, they are eternal processes. And, as we step back from this mystery, we can begin to see that, in this way, whatever our beliefs, we may truly be everlasting things.

# Death and society and truth and fairy tale

# 21

# Death:
# Worth Living For

ಬಿಂಧ

In one of the Saturday afternoons of my childhood I threw down an ace of spades in a game of cards. My partner casually observed that this was the "death card." Rather shocked at first, within moments I instinctively understood what he meant. It was black, and black, like the night, was frightening. The spade, unlike the black club, reminded one of turned dirt in gardens and cemeteries. The single spade indicated the number one, as someone once sang, "the loneliest number of all." The ace of spades was truly the death card.

In this small way, I had joined millions of people world-wide in associating death with blackness, with the consuming emptiness of our night fears. Psychoanalysts, feminists, and wordsmiths have made a lot out of the dark associations with blackness. African-Americans are sometimes described as "black as the ace of spades"—a racist reference to their not being white

85

and their resultant association with evil. The producer-director George Lucas followed an ancient tradition in his choice of costume color for *Darth Vader*. That blackness has been the home-world of vampires and werewolves, the darkness of wombs, tombs and the unconscious.

Is it any wonder that we fear death? The legends of death threaten to extinguish life, but they are also the reason for life's urgency, its hectic pace and hysteria. But real death, and dying, are not like this.

Every few weeks I meet people who come to our palliative care unit with a diagnosis of serious cancer who bring with them these infections of death imagery. They come with hearts heavy with these anxieties, and the long task of examining other ideas about death must begin just when time itself is often limited.

Will dying be slow, painful, and embarrassing? Will my passing be "difficult"? My prognosis, the time my doctor estimates that I have left, hangs over me like a curse, literally a death sentence. Like sitting on death row, the wait is excruciatingly depressing and anxiety-producing. What, if anything, can be done?

These are the kinds of questions that sit in my waiting room at work. To what horizons do we look for answers?

The prospect of death creates a sense of leaving and an enduring sense of loss. This is felt no more strongly than between young children and their parents. For adults, all but the most privileged know loss as a constant companion in life. Loss was there when you left the country of your youth. It was there when you separated and divorced, when you were retrenched, at the aftermath of the suicide of your friend or child, or the failure of your dreams of professional success. Loss rides with you. Grief is like happiness and love. They are experiences that almost everyone remembers from early in life. And they are all there—good and bad—at the end of life. Loss looms large if you haven't been paying attention to the cycles of life, and less so if you have.

Death may come suddenly, not gradually, no matter what your diagnosis. Many people die suddenly, because of the cancer, or the treatment, or for reasons we don't understand. The people you think you may be leaving behind may leave you first.

I remember talking to a man in a Sydney hospice who told me he had two friends who drove across the Nullarbor from Perth to say good-bye to him, only to be killed on their way back to Western Australia. The sad irony was that he was saying good-bye to them, but they didn't know it. Who was in the better situation, I wonder?

Surveys consistently reveal that most people want to "die in their sleep." But other studies show that death without warning is the most traumatic death for friends and family left behind.

Dying is a physical journey that is well controlled these days. Palliative medical and nursing care ensure that most people die in reasonable comfort. But no dying is easy and some dying may be difficult. But this is not news, is it? Life is difficult and, if you value it, you understand the difficult and try to rise to the occasion as best you are able, with the best friends and loved ones you are able to muster, and with as much courage and hope as you can find within yourself. That's the way it is with all deeply personal troubles. Death is absolutely no different because, despite rumors to the contrary, dying is part of life.

As for prognosis, the speculation of doctors about your life expectancy, it is wise to keep their ideas in perspective. Life expectancies are calculated on averages. A person who has *this* kind of cancer, which has spread *so* far, and responded poorly to *this* drug, but well to *that* one, will live *so* long. Often such predictions are wrong. People die much earlier. Or much later. Eventually, we all die, with or without someone handing us a prognosis.

The two health promotion workers in my unit who lead groups had both been told by doctors that they would die soon.

Joel is still working with me ten years after his prognosis. And Gail is alive and well eight years after hers. If you want to read about how long you will live, read your own autobiography not a medical text.

You may get killed on the way to work. You may have a fatal allergic response to an herb in a risotto you have just tried for the first time. You may be shot and killed in a botched hold-up attempt. These are not glib observations about how death can surprise anyone. Statistical chance is a commonly misunderstood phenomenon. It is a reliable tool of prediction for populations, but not for individual cases—not for a person and his or her particular genetics, character or social activities.

There are also people whose work, marriage, or sexual life is so depressing that they will put a hose from the car exhaust into their driver's compartment right now. If there is anything sadder than the threat of death, surely it must be the inner conviction of a healthy person that they do not *want* to live.

These things are true. Most of them are more certain than any medical prognosis. Most people are dimly aware of these everyday risks, but it does not weigh them down because they don't believe it will happen to them. If that is denial, it's a good one to have. Because if you worried about everything that might befall you, you would eventually not want to live. But shit happens. Then we must deal with it and move on.

It is personal courage and hope that give each day its purpose and help turn an ace of spades into an ace of hearts. Eventually the game will be up because each of us has to go home wherever that may be. The trick is to play well with whatever cards you are dealt. It's called living and dying well—something worth doing, perhaps, even an experience worth having.

# 22

# Death and
# Social Attitudes

ഇറങ

Have you noticed how everyone seems to have an opinion about death? There are arguments for and against having an abortion, favoring euthanasia, or believing in life after death. People become judgmental about suicide, fighting cancer, or contracting HIV. Even experimenting with ouija boards to contact the dead is no parlor game any more. "Pictionary" or "Nintendo" is seen as more neutral moral territory. And although it is not unusual to have an opinion about everything, particularly in a culture of talk-back radio, the moralism and belligerence of those opinions are an interpersonal traffic hazard for those who face death and loss on a daily basis.

Consider the subject of near-death experiences. You can find books that claim that near-death experiences are the work of the devil, yet another example of the wiles of Satan in leading humanity away from the sunny side of God. If you think that's funny, there is another whole literature arguing that there is no God, no life after death for near-death experiences to reveal, and no conscious self either. We are an illusion to ourselves. In that context, experiences are of secondary importance. Your thoughts are a self-serving device designed by your brain to give you the impression of a self. You are a type of holograph.

Or consider the experience of living with a chronic life-threatening illness. Rejecting myths abound for people living with AIDS or cancer. It is still too common to encounter the view that the disease is somehow the person's "fault." I have listened to a hospital social worker tell me that depression about cancer is caused by a "lack of faith in God." Another person with cancer tells me that her sisters instructed her not to tell anyone she has cancer—so *they* can avoid the "shame." On the other hand, other people have told me that being present at a death was "beautiful." Beautiful? What have I been missing all these years if death is beautiful? Where have I been? Has my sorrow and that of countless others been mere reaction formation—a defense mechanism that makes an emotion express itself as the opposite? If there are people who view death as beautiful, then be afraid. Be very afraid.

And then there are people who grieve who are told by others that they "will get over it." If they don't look like they are "getting over it," they may just as quickly be told to "get help." No one says to you at the funeral, just as the coffin is lowered into the grave or into the furnace, that, "your time begins now." You have exactly six months to look normal again or we call the counselors. "Neighborhood Watch" has a new meaning: Look good or be helped.

Most of these views, and the strength and personal power behind them, come from people's belief about where certainty can be found in life. Today, that's a toss-up between scientific humanism, or religion in its New Age or traditional guises.

And that's because both of these influences have a strong cultural impact on people's attitudes toward death.

As an undergraduate reading the history and philosophy of science, we all marveled at how religion in the Middle Ages readily pronounced on scientific matters. This was an early sign of rot in the church, and the arrogance was to lead to a credibility gap from which the church is still arguably recovering. But have you noticed how many science writers today are pronouncing on the (non)existence of God, the nature of evil, or the (im)possibility of human survival beyond death?

When Columbus sailed for the Americas, the "experts" said the earth was flat. Nice call, fellas! When Einstein argued that space was curved, "scientific meetings" were held to argue that this was nonsense. It was not science or religion, however, that was the problem then or now, but slavish attachment to certainty. The children's writer Carl Ewald tells a fairy tale about a fairy tale which illustrates the point well.

Once upon a time, Truth suddenly vanished from the world. Five wise men were sent out to search for it. They were away a long time but eventually each returned jubilantly to announce that he had found Truth. The first man said that Truth had changed its name and was now called Science. Another man declared this to be nonsense and announced that Theology was the truth. Yet another of the wise men announced that Love was the truth but a fourth man shouted him down naming Gold as truth's identity. The last man announced that Wine was the truth. At that point a large and noisy argument broke out with people taking various sides.

Away from the fracas, a few people sat alone and mourned that Truth had gone to pieces and would never be made whole again. But suddenly amid all the noise and fighting came the voice of a little girl who said she believed that she knew the whereabouts of Truth. She led the people to a small meadow where, in the center, surrounded by a clearing of small flowers and low grass, stood an amazing figure. Ewald describes this figure as not man or woman, child or adult, but with a mysterious combination of all their characteristics. Its eyes were deep and serious but with an obvious warmth and friendliness. It seemed to be sad and yet it smiled brightly on those who gazed at it. Its bodily features seemed at once to be soft yet firm. It walked the earth without crushing that beneath it and appeared to have long soft wings. When it drew itself erect it cried, making sounds like ringing bells. When finally it chose to speak it simply said, "I am Truth." This announcement was immediately greeted by Science, Love, Theology, Gold, and Wine unanimously and in one voice. "It's a fairy tale!" they all said.

If we could be certain about everything, there would be need for argument, especially scientific argument. If we could be certain about everything, we would not need to be followers—especially religious followers. The prevailing uncertainty in life means that we often too quickly place our faith in these things. This often results in a complete and shameless lack of humility and the ready and comfortable use of prejudiced thinking about mysteries, including death. The fairy tale about the fairy tale is about the loss of humility in our search for truth, both within and outside ourselves.

There are few ready answers to the most important questions about death—Is it ever "right" to take my own life? Can I continue to live meaningfully carrying grief in my heart? Can I ever forgive another for the death of someone I love? Who will dry my tears? Will we ever meet again?—and they are never the same for everyone who asks them. Anyone who tells you differently may be trying to sell you something. Buyer beware. Because our needs are so different from one another, *all* things need to be considered. You must take from each what you will. But remember, and remember to tell others, you are looking for meaning not membership.

# 23

# Public Notice

ॐ

WARNING: Those ill or grieving should note that social dangers lie in these waters. To avoid hazards, unfamiliar persons should swim with attitude.

The experience of serious illness or loss can encourage other people to take an inordinate and unhealthy interest in your affairs. All sorts of people suddenly seem to feel free to call upon you, providing you with unwanted attention or opinion. The idea of death combines both fame and misfortune to most people and the reaction of people to you is something to be seriously negotiated.

Consider the word "denial." In all social circles, the term denial is now liberally deployed to describe any reluctance to speak about death. Although the term was originally used in psycho-analytic circles to describe initial defensive reactions to the news or prospect of death, the term has well and truly broken away from that confinement. The word is now officially a feral animal.

People who do not cry in public after the death of loved ones, or at the very least do not look as sad as other people feel they should, are sometimes said to be in "denial." There are people who never talk about the prospect of death with anyone who is not a close friend or lover. Frustrated at their reluctance to discuss their feelings, some people view these recalcitrants as in denial. Other people, in their efforts to stay positive, attempt to avoid all negative thoughts, sometimes including the topic of death. Some of these people are viewed as people in denial. Yet other people with extensive disease, read about cancer cures in popular books and magazines even into their late admission into hospices. These people have also been open to charges of death-denial. In other words, people who are reserved and private, others who are attempting to employ the power of positive thinking, and others who eternally court hope are prime candidates for the pitiful label of denial. Be warned.

And while we are on the topic of denial there is also the common attempt to deny you your dignity. The warning signs come in the form of the individual who refers to you in the plural. For example, "How are we today?" "We seem sad this week," and, my favorite, "Are we certain we don't want to talk about this?" What seems increasingly clear from the anthropological evidence is that these people, when confronted with others who are ill or in distress, go into parent, big brother, or big sister mode. Whichever they choose, the news will not be good for you. If one of them adopts the role of parent or big sister, you will be the child or younger sibling. Coming from a near stranger, the result will not be a pretty picture.

The problem of being patronized can get worse particularly if you find yourself institutionalized for a time in a hospital, hospice, or nursing home. It is still not clear whether your wearing of pajamas or their wearing of uniforms brings out the worst in people. Forget the NIL BY MOUTH signs, NIL BY EAR placards would have greater use in these places.

It is common to lament the way older people in nursing homes are hostage to poor quality, patronizing, and often intrusive entertainment. We deplore how they are often treated as children, but we should see this behavior as an extension of the widespread tendency of some people to assume inadequacy in those they believe are vulnerable to advancing age, life-threatening illness, or grief and loss. Some people stereotype others instead of taking the time to listen afresh to new people that they meet. Sometimes parents and adult children will see illness or grief as a time to impose or reverse the roles of dependency when this may be the last thing the other party wants. Someone here may not be listening or watching enough.

Gloria Stuart's story is instructive. In the 1930s she played opposite such film luminaries as Eddie Cantor, Lionel Barrymore, and Shirley Temple. Then part of the glitterati of Hollywood, she would frequently be seen at dinners with Humphrey Bogart or Groucho Marx. She made forty-two films and *Screenplay Magazine* voted her one of Hollywood's top ten beauties in the 1930s. After the birth of her first child, Gloria gave the film-star business away. Fed up with being in B- and C-grade movies she traveled and went into business instead. No one in the movie-watching world heard of her again until a late comeback in the role of Old Rose in the film *Titanic*. She was nominated for an Oscar, for best supporting actress. So what, you might say, just another movie star comeback story. Not quite. Gloria's triumphant story is not about comebacks.

Gloria loved the film-making game, but she could never break into the A-list of stars. Her good looks seemed to doom her to playing "cheesecake" roles in lesser films. She never felt that she got the opportunity to experience acclaim for her work, not mere fame but acclaim—an appreciation for her acting ability. There was always a lingering sense of doubt and missed opportunity that seemed to stay with her until given the role of Old Rose by the firm's director James Cameron.

In a *Daily Telegraph* interview with Charles Laurence, Gloria describes her late opportunity as like "being saved"—but from what? Gloria was saved from being eternally typecast. In the first place, she had been typecast as "cheese-cake." In other words, beauty cannot act. Beauty is talentless. Her Oscar nomination put paid to that. In the second, she had been typecast as "old," and being old meant being "finished." But, as film history has shown, Gloria was not finished.

Most of us can learn from Gloria's story. Gloria suffered for years by being unfairly typecast. Because of her beauty, or later her advanced age, some people assumed her to be inadequate in some way. This typecasting acted as an invisible social barrier to others, preventing them from giving Gloria the benefit of the doubt. And so it is with labeling others in general but here, of course, I particularly refer to the idea of denial and other strange reactions to people in distress.

Facing the possibility of death, or experiencing grief, does not automatically mean that we need to share our troubles, doubts or fears with anyone who offers or who happens by. You and I share our troubles only with those people that we choose for that purpose. We may also choose to hope when others do not. But the choice is always ours.

# 24

# A History Lesson

ಬಂಚ

One of the most common questions that people ask when facing death or bereavement is "Why me?" Why, at the age of forty-five, have I been diagnosed with HIV, or cardiac failure, or cancer? Why me? Everyone else seems so well. The future looks so normal and bright for them. Why have my family and I been singled out for this tragedy, this inexplicable dagger to the heart, this slow dying in the mid-summer of life?

Until the beginning of the twentieth century, most people did not ask these questions. Death was widely viewed as a normal and frequently occurring event. Life expectancy for most of human history was in the low twenties. When the remains of the first Neanderthal Man were discovered in a European cave site, it was widely reported and celebrated. Neanderthal Man was discovered with food remnants, hunting implements, and other personal affects, indications that his people might have entertained a belief in personal survival of death. What was less widely known was that Neanderthal "Man" was a boy of seventeen years of age. For most of human history death was mainly the experience of infants, children, and young people.

In Europe in the Addle Ages, death was widely viewed as a supernatural person, a grim reaper, who had a particular taste for children. Infant mortality was so high that part of the reason for having large families was so that some of the children might survive into adulthood. Many children were not named until they were three or four years old and when they reached that age were quickly dressed as adults so that "death" did not recognize them as children. Death was also common among adults.

War and infectious diseases were a normal part of human affairs. Accidents on farms were common. Unsafe building construction led to many deaths from housing collapse. Poor animal husbandry practices, unclean food storage and preparation, polluted sources of drinking water, and inadequate sewerage led to a very high rate of deadly infections among adults. Among tribal peoples, peasants, and later the industrial working classes, people lived so closely together that death was commonly and widely witnessed by all family members.

In the twentieth century, there were important social improvements to living standards: public health rose, there was better housing, sewerage and water systems, there were improvements in medical care and workplace safety, and a general increase in disposable income. Life expectancy began to rise sharply. In simple health terms, the quality of life improved rapidly for most people in industrialized societies. As people had more to spend, their housing, improved and privacy also became valued.

The unpleasantness of sickness, disability, and death started to be dealt with by institutions such as hospitals, nursing homes, or funeral companies. Our personal experience of death fell away. When death occurs now, there are few people to whom we can turn to ask for advice or from whom we can learn.

Most people are in the same situation or have even less experience than us. This is the modern context of facing death.

I once conducted a study of castaways. I read dozens of
accounts written by survivors of this kind of ordeal. These
were people who were often on yachting expeditions and whose
ship had foundered in bad weather or had collided with a
surfacing whale. Consistently their accounts resembled those of
people who reported near-death experiences. They would report
out-of-body sensations, for example. In the loneliness of their
predicament they were often compelled to review their lives.
Other people reported meeting supernatural beings or being
visited by deceased relatives or friends. Rescue was welcome
but often unexpected, occurring as it often did after a long period
at sea when their expectations of dying were greater than the
belief that they would see land again. During my research I
came across another book which assembled similar accounts
of isolation after shipwrecks in the eighteenth and nineteenth
centuries. What struck me about these accounts was that none
reported any mystical experiences at all. Why was this?

For modern castaways, the prospect of death comes as a
shock. People in our time expect to see their old age, not die at
sea in mid life. For ancient mariners, on the other hand, the
prospect of death was hardly riveting. Death was not necessarily
a topic that concentrated the mind. These people had grown up
with death, knew it well in adulthood, and expected it sooner
rather than later for themselves. The question was never
"Why me?" but "When me?"

The lesson we can learn from the apparent loneliness of
modern dying is not how more personally wounding this
experience is from previous periods—it is not—but how our
lack of experience with these human verities aggravates those
wounds. The modern prospect of death, or the experience of
grief, leads us to feel that we have been singled out by fate.
Paradoxically, because death now seems to work shorter hours

than it ever did, its appearance on our doorstep feels more cruel and more personal than in any previous time.

And it's true, death has become more personal. We are now forced to think about the individual meaning of our losses and our lives more than ever before. We are forced to concentrate our minds on the preciousness of each other as no time in previous history. And we are forced more than any time in our human history to view death as a crisis of personal development and spiritual possibility. The church no longer tells us how to make sense of death. Medicine and science have not helped us here either. The task of making meaning from our life and death often falls personally to each of us, person to person. Death is no blessing, but in modern times its personal impact can propel you toward unexpected lessons and valuable personal insights. The cruelty of death today may be in the spurning of them.

# 25

# Room for a View

ഉറ

I have never been a great traveler until recently, and even then, not a very keen one. I'm a bit of a home-body really. But this doesn't mean that I don't have places that are special to me around the globe. I love St. Paul's Cathedral in London, for example. Every time I go to London I always make sure that I have a spare hour to go there. My partner has "seen" St. Paul's enough times now and so she doesn't come with me. I go by myself. I pay for my ticket to go right to the top. From there I feel that I can see all of London. I stand cross-armed leaning on the wrought-iron railing and stare out at the view. Sometimes I am asked to take someone's picture because I appear alone, am stationary for long enough for many to notice me, and perhaps look affable enough for them to ask for such a favor.

After a while I descend so many hundreds of stairs and visit the crypts in the basement ramparts below. There are tombs of famous English war heroes and writers. I particularly like to visit William Blake's. He was a marvelous poet, writer, and artist who had a life-long love affair with the mysteries of life.

My climb above and below St. Paul's reminds me of life. All the action takes place in the middle of the church, not above or below it. But the above and below are vital and necessary in their own way. Above is a view, perhaps of the place of St. Paul's in the urban scheme of London or its place in English society and ideas. Below is a reminder of our final destinies. Here lies the physical reminder of our destinations however great or small. Above is hope and perspective. Below is the reality of death and the useful reminder that time is short and we must all do what we must do. I love St. Paul's. I love its inspirational architecture. I love the view from there.

I was recently at a conference in the tiny Republic of San Marino, in Italy. San Marino is only 65 square miles in size but has been an independent nation on top of towering hill-tops for centuries. San Marino overlooks the Italian city of Rimini, an urban center with its feet dangling into the Adriatic Sea.

When I checked into my hotel room and walked out to my terrace, I saw a beautiful multi-layered scene of mountains. Between each set of mountains were valleys of low mist, which had settled there as the day undressed into evening. When the sun set over those mountains, I could see part of the reason why the people of San Marino had fought so hard for their independence. There is something in a majestic view that is breathtaking and nourishing for a weary or distressed soul. And it is easy to see how a good view of your homeland can renew the heart of any nationalist.

Often when people find themselves in crisis, particularly when they are ill or bereaved, they develop an interest in religious or philosophical writings. Some people look with interest, for the first time, at New Age books. Some look again at their Bible. Others develop an interest in theories of health drawn from broader philosophies, such as Chi Qung, Shiatsu, Yoga, or transcendental meditation.

Many health care professionals, and many others who are themselves ill or bereaved, look at such interest with suspicion. But it may be short-sighted. We are concerned about the practical usefulness of such reading, even the possible harm. And it is right to be wary of things that may harm us when they pose as something that may help. What really seems to worry them, however, is not the content of the material but the new interest in these ideas from people who have not previously shown it before. We are concerned at their changed behavior. But how interested are we in the positive value they might gain from this excursion?

Perhaps during any crisis, as in any travel, there is use for a room with a view. Religious writings or broader philosophical writings may give people that room. And views help us to gain a sense of perspective, to better locate ourselves in the scheme of things. They can also nourish the soul, by which I mean they can help lift your morale by taking you outside your tormented self for a moment, or maybe longer. This can allow you to "see" the bigger picture, and by doing so, give you the strength to continue to endure, survive, and see beyond the confines of your situation.

When traveling we are wise not to underestimate the power of a good view. If you know of one, go and have a look. Be careful, of course, but look anyway. You never know what you might see from there.

# 26

# Visitor to No. 23

ॐ

The strongest statement of security, safety, and care in the 150 psalms in the Bible comes from Psalm 23. And what makes it particularly dramatic, and also very poignant, is its coming hard on the heels of Psalm 22—passages which give voice to cries of dereliction, of abandonment. Out of these former depths of despair and self-doubt Psalm 23 emerges, like a solitary musical note growing slowly more loudly. As we read each new word, flickers of light cast themselves onto our beleaguered souls.

> The Lord is my shepherd. I shall not want.
> He maketh me lie down in green pastures: he leadeth me beside the still waters.
> He restoreth my soul. He leadeth me in the paths of righteousness for his name's sake.
> Yea, though I walk through the valley of the shadow of death, I will fear no evil: for thou art with me; thy rod and thy staff comfort me. Thou preparest a table before one in the presence of mine enemies: thou anointest my head with oil, my cup runneth over.
> Surely goodness and mercy will follow me all the days of my life: and I will dwell in the house of the Lord forever.

This is a striking song, its words stunning in their power. To me their ultimate reference—to God the shepherd—is foreign. I do not, for example, respond to the medieval pastoral image. Yet there is much in these words that I find striking and comforting.

In the early years of my childhood, my family lived in working-class areas far from the center of Sydney. The houses were built of fibro-cement and the roads were dirt with no cerbing or guttering. In those days, there was no town sewerage system and men would come around every few days with soil-carts to remove the human waste from backyard toilets. Unemployment was a steady feature of the social landscape just as violence was part of the domestic one. Few trees existed and no gardens could be seen where I lived. The landscape was dry and dusty and abandoned car hulks sat like dead animals in front yards or in the local playground.

And then one day my mother got a job, just for a few months, as a housekeeper to a widow living in a wealthy inner-city suburb overlooking Sydney Harbor. Mrs. McBride lived in a home that looked like a doll's house. It had a low sandstone fence covered in purple lantana creeper. Flowers grew along the sides of her front and backyard. There was even a small vegetable garden. Along the street and inside neighbor's yards there were trees, some of which even flowered. Inside Mrs. M's house, there were clocks and sofas, and paintings and appliances that I had never seen before. And when she had visitors they came in new cars, many of which had leather seats and walnut-wood dashboards. As far as I could tell, Mrs. McBride lived in heaven.

I loved Mrs. M's world, but I knew that I was only a visitor. This was not where I belonged. But even then I knew that what I loved about Mrs. M's house was not so much the lovely furniture and surroundings but the promise they held out to me. I learned that my world was only one world. Life could be full of beautiful objects. There were other ways of doing things, other ways of living. At six years of age I became an early but admiring visitor to possibility. It was not the facts of material comfort and wealth that impressed me so much as my realization of their existence.

It was not the possibility that I might have such a life one day that impressed me. (I did not imagine that I would.) But that Mrs. M's world, for all its wonder, co-existed with my own. This amazed me. And just as some people are bitten by the "travel bug" I was, from those days, taken by the idea of possibility. If there were cars with walnut-wood dashboards in the world, what other wonders awaited me?

And so it is with Psalm 23. Although an icon of Christian worship, burdened in parts by medieval imagery and archaic language, the song is an impressive testimony to personal faith. Not faith in churches or organized religions; not faith in religious history, but a simple and beautiful faith in an endangered human species—hope. As a visitor to No. 23 you quickly realize that this is a soliloquy, something you say (or sing) to yourself. You are encouraged to participate in the possibility that you are an important living being and that, present trials notwithstanding, you can triumph over them. You have overcome difficulties before, not always as you might have anticipated, but you might and do so again. It is okay, and it makes sense, to hope.

Although formal religion may no longer be part of your world, if it ever was, this does not mean that such traditions are not living and breathing and do not have things of everlasting value to you. Religious texts, because their sources of inspiration are often derived from human trials and suffering, do contain valuable ideas, and only prejudice would spurn them. Sometimes sources of insight and comfort come from strange and unexpected places. Psalm 23 reminds us that hope and despair co-exist in the same world—your world—which is comforting to remember at times of difficulty and despair.

And when it comes to readily available sites of hope, such as those at No. 23, visitors are always welcome. Who knows, you might even move in and stay.

# 27

# Not Fate

ಏಿೂ

The Irish have a folktale that highlights their belief in the role of fate in the timing of death. Entitled "No Man Goes Beyond His Day," it goes something like this.

A boat with several men was going out to a reef to fish from those rocks when the men realized that they had left their mast behind. They turned back and after a while arrived at the cove of their village. When they arrived, they met an old friend fishing from the pier and asked him if he would like to join them on their fishing expedition. He was delighted to be asked and soon joined them on the boat. Away they sailed and upon arriving at the reef the men spread out along the rocks.

At the end of the day's fishing, the owner of the boat roamed the reef to collect the men for the return trip home. All the men were found except the man who joined them late. He had been fishing at the rear of the reef, on the wilder side. The remnants of his gear were washed over a large area. The fisherman was nowhere to be seen and it soon became clear that he had been dragged into the sea by a rogue wave. He was never seen again. So, although the fishermen thought they were returning for the mast, they were really returning for the man who was later lost. No man goes beyond his day.

But there are other ways to tell the story.

A boat with several men were going out to a reef to fish from those rocks when they realized that they had left their mast behind. They turned back and after a while arrived at the cove of their village. When they arrived there, they met an old friend fishing from the pier and asked him if he would like to join them on their fishing expedition to the reef. He was delighted to be asked and soon joined the rest of them on the boat. Away they sailed again. Halfway there, they met another boat coming back from the reef.

Apparently, while the first boat was retrieving its mast, a perilous squall developed over the sea near the reef and several fishing boats and their occupants were drowned. Even on the second boat, several sailors had lost their lives. The surviving crew warned those in the first boat to return to the safety of the cove. So, although the fishermen thought they were returning for the mast, they were really participants in a chance journey to save their own lives. No man was chained to his day.

But there are still other ways to tell the story.

A boat with several men was going out to a reef to fish from those rocks when they realized that they had left their mast behind. They turned back and after a while arrived at the cove of their village. When they got there, they met an old friend fishing from the pier and asked him if he'd like to join them on their fishing expedition to the reef. He was delighted to be asked and soon joined the rest of them on the boat. Away they sailed again and, upon arriving at the reef, all spread out along the rocks at different locations. At the end of the day's fishing, the owner of the boat roamed the reef to collect all the men for the return trip home. All of them were found except the man who joined them late. Eventually they discovered the place where the man had been fishing at the rear of the reef, on the wilder side. The remnants of his gear were washed over a large area. The fisherman was nowhere to be seen and it became obvious that he had been dragged into the sea by a rogue wave.

They returned to their village and informed the lost man's family. The next day the fishermen and the lost man's friends and family sailed out to the reef for a memorial service. When they reached the reef, they were all startled to be greeted by the "lost man." He had been washed off the rocks that day and the strong currents and rips in the sea had kept him from reaching shore at the spot where he had been washed away. By the time he managed to reach the shore, wet and exhausted, it was nightfall and his friends had long left the reef. He stayed there all night and day sheltering among the rocks and eating seaweed and any small fish or crab that he could catch until they returned. So, although the fishermen thought they were returning for a memorial service, they were returning for the man himself.

Some men survive their day.

But there are still other ways to tell the story.

A boat with several men were going out to a reef to fish from those rocks when they realized that they had left their mast behind. They turned back and after a while arrived at the cove of their village. When they arrived there, they meet an old friend fishing from the pier and asked him if he'd like to join them on their fishing expedition to the reef. He was delighted to be asked and soon joined the rest of them on the boat. Away they sailed again and upon arriving at the reef all spread out along the rocks at different locations.

At the end of the day's fishing, the owner of the boat roamed the reef to collect the men to return home. All of them were found except the man who joined them late. Eventually they found the place where the man had been last seen fishing. But he was nowhere to be seen and it was obvious that he had been dragged into the sea by a rogue wave. They returned home to tell the grim news to the man's wife and children. The fishermen, caps in hand, gathered at the door of his home and told his wife the sad news. The wife was distressed to hear their story. The fishermen must have been mistaken she pleaded, because her husband, the devoted fisherman, died the night before. So, although the fishermen thought they were returning for the mast, it turned out that they were returning for a specter who would never turn down an offer of a good place to fish.

Some men die but do not go beyond.

Let me ask you this question: in which story are appearances not what they seem? Answer: all of them. In the last story, of course, the "fisherman" turns out to be a ghost. In the third story, the "lost" man turns out to be a survivor. In the second story, the irritation of someone's forgetfulness turned something which was-to-be into something which was not-to-be. The initial problem of forgetting the mast turns out to be everyone's good fortune.

And the first, original story? The last three stories show us that the message of the first one underestimates our personal role in each other's destinies. The first story is not simply about a rogue wave, but the story of how one fisherman's decision led him to a meeting with that wave. If tales of survival by struggle or by human error have messages in common with ghost stories it is this: Some people may go beyond their day. And if they do continue to live and breathe, and even if they don't, that power is always in their own hands or those of others. But not absolutely, entirely, or wholly with this impersonal idea that some have come to call "fate."

# 28

# Life and Death

ಇಂದ

There are 477 gods of death in Marjorie Leach's world-encyclopedic *Guide to the Gods*. The Warao in Venezuela know death as Abuhene, an evil god of death who represents the setting sun. In India, Kati Ankamma is the goddess of cremation and burial who devours corpses and preys on children and cattle. In Bohemia, Morana is a goddess of death and of winter. The Chinese have a god who helps souls of the dead to the afterworld so that they may be judged. And in the Fijian Islands, Ravuravu is known as the god of murder. The list of the gods who embody death rolls on for another 472 paragraphs.

We have always named death. It helps us to recognize it, to see it coming, as it were. And to visualize it and perhaps ward it off, if we can. When we repeat the name of Kati Ankamma or of Ravuravu, we feel as if we are in some introductory college course in the anthropology of religion. We wonder at how "others" arrive at such beliefs. But it doesn't take long to see how.

Who are our powerful "gods" who steal into the night to carry our living off into the world of the dead? Who are we powerless against, those whose names send shivers down our spines?

Cancer, AIDS, neurological disease, leukemia, heart attack, and road fatality? Then there are the smaller gods. Electrocution, drowning, acute appendicitis, sudden infant death syndrome, and cystic fibrosis. Some of the smaller deities are particularly evil. Their uncommon occurrence does not lessen our fear of them—murder, suicide, bushfire, cyclone, earthquake, and tornado. All the gods of death are feared. All of them dress differently and announce themselves to their victims with different voices, some with a loud shriek and others with a chilling whisper.

Some of these gods you can see coming from your kitchen window like a tornado sweeping across the cornfields. Others creep into your insides while you are asleep at night, only announcing themselves in a new cough, pain or weakness not present the day before. Others display a most divine patience, ever so slowly invading your life by the inch, stealing just a few seconds or a minute each day, something you hardly notice. But in the mirror some mornings your face seems to change just slightly. And then you notice the difference age makes each day, each month, each year, every year. Something is draining your life away and it knows how to count.

But if any death is a demon, it shares its house inside you with a host of other gods. For what I omitted to add about Leach's wonderful *Guide to the Gods* is that the gods of life outnumber the gods of death two to one. All over the world, and in all times, it is the gods of life that dominate and make life worth living—the blessed spirits of the sky, of wind and water, and of earth, culture and work. The gods of life are more numerous in human history and culture and send a forceful message to future generations, which says that the forces of life are the important ones, perhaps the only ones. Isn't it true that the gods of death could not perform their cruel work without some life of their own?

What the gods of death cannot do without your permission is to shoplift your hope or courage, pocket your joy-in-the-moment, or rob you of enduring love. If these things are to be given up in aging, dying or loss, it is you who hand them over. And if you give these things up, you have died already, or will soon. Why would you do *that* willingly? All over the world the multicultural faces of death know these gifts are yours for keeps. So don't hand them over, because when they go, so do you. Keep them close. And when the dark ones call, turn your back on them, not on life.

# 29

# LOSS

ഇൻരു

Some people unconsciously draw a distinction between their own loss and other people's losses. When indigenous people angrily demand the return of their artifacts from museums, for example, we sometimes struggle to understand the depth of their grief. How can a concern for some small physical item be the source of so much pain? Events over which they mourn happened so long ago. But loss is loss. Big losses are re-opened by smaller ones, and sometimes the smaller ones are embodied in little objects.

When I was five, my mother and I returned to Japan because her Australian marriage had broken up. Sadly, we were not welcome. At my Grandma's house, the eldest son beat my mother and I and threw our luggage onto the street outside. My mother had shamed the house by bringing home a mixed-race child. My mother's cousin and her husband took us into their house until we could find our own accommodation, but I always remembered that the decision to take us in resided with the man of the house and not my mother's female cousin. Shinjiro was blind. And he did not see that I was European-looking. When he ran his hands over my face to "see" me he only saw a child. And I only saw that he was a man of great kindness.

We returned to Australia not long after and over the years I received nothing from any part of my mother's family. No birthday cards or presents. No letters. No phone calls. After a while it was no different from simply having no family. But that was okay because I had a wonderful mother and close friends who were like brothers and sisters to me. I had these riches then as I still do now. But one day, after all the racists in my family had died, my mother returned to Japan. And when she got back to Australia, she brought me a gift from an auntie who lived in the country. I was so surprised and, though I said little at the time, I felt deeply grateful for this small thing—whatever it was.

When I opened the gift, I found that it was a Japanese flag. It was an old one with leather corners on one side where it should be hung. It had been folded for a long time and obviously water had seeped into the wrapping because leather stains had appeared on other parts of the largely white flag. I handled it carefully and looked to Mum for an explanation. My aunt was in her eighties. When she was a young woman she was in love with a young man who was about to go to war. He gave her this flag to remind her of him until his return. He never did.

She learned to love another but always kept this flag in a secret place. Her husband never knew of its existence. Getting old, and for reasons best known only to her, she gave this flag with its story to my mother to give to me. The reason that she gave ME the gift remains a mystery to me, but its connection to her earlier love and loss over a young man made it profoundly special to me. I cannot write more words about this.

I had the flag for several years. I always kept it folded away and would take it out to look at now and again. One day when we moved from that house, it was suddenly and inexplicably lost. I suspect that one of the removalists, who was strangely using towels and sheets to wrap other household items, discovered the flag, realized its age and authenticity, and took it for a souvenir. Perhaps it sits in someone's living room as a curio and talking piece, no one realizing its rightful place in the heart and spirit of two people who grieve for what it meant to each of them.

In the 1920s, the children's writer Monica Shannon wrote a charming fairy tale about a little girl who meets a boy who is very good at finding things. Impressed with his own skill, he asks the girl what she would like him to find for her. She asks him to find a dream, a lost dream. She had it only once, and although she had never seen it again, she had never forgotten it. I know how she feels. I think we all do. Loss is loss.

# 30

# Eternity and Me

ဆာထၜ

I know that I shouldn't do this, but I just can't seem to help myself. As my walking companion and I stroll through a delightful Sydney park lined with Moreton Bay fig trees, something is said that makes me feel so very glad. I lift my arms straight out by my sides, throw back my head, and suddenly lift my whole body horizontally into the air. Within moments I am soaring above the trees and above my friend, and slowly moving across the park with a gentle breeze blowing through my hair. I know very well that this is astonishing behavior and that if anyone in the cars below see me they will quickly use their mobile phone to call the media. I can just see the scandal sheet headlines now: "Real Life X-File: Professor Flies."

My university will ask me to explain, no doubt, but at this time I couldn't care less. I spot two other friends walking along a path. Our eyes meet, but they are not surprised. They wave gaily at me as I fly past them. And look! There's the old corner shop where my school friends and I used to buy sugar-sherbets after school. Incredible. And look at that! The sky looks so blue and affectionate today. Good flying weather, if you must. I open my eyes and peer weakly at the clock—7.34 AM. Oh no, another dream. Where *does* the brain get this stuff?

Sometimes my waking life is just as inexplicable to me as my sleeping one. There was a time when, like many people, I had a job that I hated. The people I worked with didn't seem to like me. Those who ruled the workplace made sure no benefits came my way. The handful of friends that I had there were treated in the same way. We were the out-group. Any interest that my friends and I expressed in desirable positions or activities was met with barely muffled hysteria and hastily assembled back-room meetings. These workplace performances occur everywhere, for their own reasons, against the perceived enemies of good social order, for the benefit of those who believe they hold the precarious sanity and safety of the workplace in their own hands. In other workplaces, I have been part of the in-group, but alas, not at this one. That, as they say, is the luck of the draw.

One day during that time, as I drove interstate to a conference, I steered the car a hundred kilometers off course and made my way to a vast inland lake system that was fed through a narrow sand-bar entry by the open sea. I stopped the car and took off my shoes and socks. I sat on the sand with my feet in several inches of salty water watching small choppy waves wash over the lower parts of my legs. As I looked around at the lonely sand dunes and the shallow seawater in front, I suddenly felt happy. The water on my legs was cold, sobering, tickling. I felt that I could see more sharply than normal, stimulated by the coldness of the water and the vast openness of the scenery around me.

I threw sand in the water absentmindedly and gazed at distant birds swooping over some dunes nearby. I was content. And really glad that I had taken this diversion. At that moment I wished that I could build a little house, right here by the water's edge, and stay here for who knows how long. I thought about my work colleagues and the workplace politics, which colored my everyday experience. In this place all those things seemed far away, did not appear to be real. It was like a bad dream, happening to someone else.

What was real was now. The seashore on my legs. Yet I knew that, worse luck, if anything was a dream it was where I was now, on that sand. But on that beach I was compelled, as after any surreal bedtime dream, to ask about my life at work: where does life get this stuff? How is it that I can do so little to stop the culture at work that seems so determined to get the better of me?

In these ways, my flying dream and the other events in my life seem difficult to control. These are not events or experiences that I knowingly create. I have a small, perhaps even important, measure of influence over them, but the worlds of my dreams, like the twentieth century, are not of my conscious creation. And yet in each of these experiences I am there as Me. I make my choices to fly above the park, choosing to acknowledge the social consequences, or to argue against colleagues, knowing the interpersonal and political consequences of generating conflict in a professional but parochial culture. I am *inside* these many events and I continue to choose.

Humanist psychologists such as Rollo May and Carl Rogers once argued that we are made human by our choices. Between the determinism of environment and endowment, our personal decisions blow on the dice, thereby influencing the outcome, however feebly. I make the choices and the choices make me. And I am inside those choices, inside the workplace where you can see me, inside my brain where you cannot.

Perhaps my choices do more than make me human. Perhaps they make me real, make me *experience* what I am, what *I* actually is. These confront me with what it means to be an individual like me. In illness and loss, perhaps also in the transition of death, as in all other transitions in life, I might continue to make those choices. And if I continue to make those choices, they will undoubtedly continue to "make" me. Through these conscious acts, I might continue to be real and present in my life and in those of others.

Surely this is what the mystics mean when they talk about transcendence. This living and choosing self is clearly an existence beyond the mere mortal currents of circumstance and synapses, simultaneously planted inside of, and yet somehow above, the dreamy reality of life itself. Maybe it is here—in this partly submerged and partly separate self—that we see some genuine path that leads away from that reality, a glimpse of eternity, perhaps even, of a promise of things unseen.

# Secrets of the clasped hands of the heart

# 31

# Grief

၍

When I was browsing in an old church bookshop one year, I came across a small forty-eight page book published in 1908. It was simply called, *Thysia: An Elegy*. The pages were brown with age, and there was only one photograph, at the beginning of the book, opposite the title page. The photograph was a small black and white plate of what appeared to be the shaded area beneath a large tree on a hillside. But beneath the photo the caption read: "Nothing to mark it but a little mound." The author of this remarkable book chose to remain anonymous.

I was nineteen years old when I stumbled upon this book. At the time, my main concerns were the whereabouts of my next hamburger, university assignment, or girlfriend. Grief and loss were far from my mind. But the lonely clarity of the grief, which whispered to me in this volume, so hidden among other books, resonated deep inside me, compelling me to buy it. This was not great literature, let me tell you. But in the awkward rhymes of the author's poetry, the tortured lines of someone's private grief over the death of his wife came to me with the power and tenderness of something that might have been written only the day before. The tears that entered my heart that day as I read the first pages swept into me as if someone were weeping them before me.

I kept this book with me wherever I went and even today I cannot read its little passages without being moved. It uncovers my own life's pains and loss, leaving me momentarily immobilized before their power.

In the palliative care unit, I frequently talk to the elderly, the bereaved, the terminally ill, or war veterans, and the theme that recurs in these conversations is that grief is death to a part of the self. And it does not grow back. Grief does not "heal." You do *not* get over loss. And it never stops hurting. You can always play "hide and seek" with feelings. There are days, even years, when those losses do not loom large in your mind. But there are other times when someone has left the lid open and you are helpless to find a way to close those feelings out.

My mother used to describe love as a preciousness found only in the heart. She would clasp her hands together and peer into the small hole made by her two parting thumbs. "When life is sad, you can peer into your heart and remember all the good things that are yours—your friends, your bottle-cap collection, your own mother," she would say with a wry smile. And it is true. But what happens when the things and people inside the clasped hands of your heart are taken from you? This is the most tragic burglary of all. And the cruelest irony is that it travels by the name of "Life."

So what happens inside your heart and to your soul? Initially, you lie broken on the ground. This is not always obvious to outsiders. Sometimes they can tell from your tears, but they are never there when you are alone, in the dark, when everyone else in town is asleep. The tears come from a deep deadness inside. This can feel like an injury inside the chest and a twisted tightness in the throat. Sometimes there is real chest pain, sometimes a dull heaviness that won't go away, the physical inspiration for the phrase "a broken heart."

The companion, or alternative to this experience, is depression. This is a sad feeling that can sometimes become anger, sometimes guilt or anxiety, but always a frustration at not being able to hold, shout, kiss, touch, or say sorry to the one dear person you have lost. And lost is precisely how all this can make you feel.

There are "good days" and "bad" ones, very bad ones. In time, you develop special psychological and social skills. You learn to think and dream about your loss by yourself. You learn to express the inexpressible to select friends, to help them understand your progress. Then mercifully, you gently let them off the hook by not mentioning your loss again, except in some abstract way—like academic reflections on the Second World War. But gradually you come to understand, in a sad and often lonely way, that this loss is yours forever. You come to realize that just as the object of your love was part of who and what you were, this new loss is part of who and what you are now. You no longer see as you saw before, no longer feel the same about some things as you once felt before. You have just discovered how the price of love is exacted on those of us who lose it.

When you listen to others who have been hurt, especially those who know loss firsthand as you do, you weep *with* them now, not *for* them. You journey with them, both as watcher and keeper over the secrets of the clasped hands of the heart. You learn, as I have learned, that what is deep inside are parts of your precious experience which have somehow become your inner eye, and part of your soul—that which, in rare moments, is able to touch another. In these moments of human connection, experiences of loss are like those of love. They can turn strangers into people who understand each other. In this way, the Athenian poet Aeschylus was right when he reminded us:

> In our sleep, pain which cannot forget
> Falls drop by drop upon the heart
> Until, in our own despair, against our will,
> Comes wisdom through the awful grace of God.

# 32

# The Legend of
# the White Butterfly

ഇരു

There is an old Japanese legend that reminds us about the power of love over death. Long ago, there lived an old man by the name of Takahama who lived alone in a small house behind a cemetery. Although never married and a bit eccentric, he was nevertheless thought to be a kind and harmless old man. In those days it was considered rather odd to live near a cemetery, and many people thought that perhaps this contributed to his isolation all those years. One summer he became quite ill and sent for his sister-in-law. She came as quickly as she could, bringing her teenage son with her for help.

They both did as much as they were able to make old man Takahama comfortable, but it was soon clear that he was dying. As Takahama slipped quietly into a final sleep, his sister-in-law and nephew keeping watch beside him, a little white butterfly entered the room and flew to Takahama's pillow. Alarmed at this strange event, the nephew attempted to shoo the butterfly away, but each time he did so the creature returned. After three failed attempts to send the butterfly away, the nephew managed to chase the butterfly out of the room and follow it into the garden.

Fearing the butterfly's return (it was a persistent creature), the nephew continued to follow the butterfly into the cemetery where it disappeared over an old weather-beaten tomb. The nephew noticed that this tomb bore the name of a girl who had died at the age of eighteen half a century earlier. This was not strange. But the grave was surrounded by fresh flowers and their little water tins had been filled quite recently.

When the nephew returned to the house, old man Takahama had passed away. The boy told his mother what he had seen. And the mother explained to her son that the grave he had seen belonged to Akiko, a young village girl who had been betrothed to Takahama but who had died of consumption only days before their wedding. Every day, and every year since that time, Takahama had gone to the cemetery to put flowers on her grave and to sweep the tomb. After some years had passed, Takahama had moved to the little house near the cemetery so that he could perform this daily act of love. When finally he could not come to her, Akiko's spirit came to collect him so that they could be reunited and begin their sweet journey together in the next world.

This legend of the white butterfly tells us about the importance and meaning of acts of remembrance—the personal devotion of attending to a place that represents the person who has died. This remembering has traditionally taken place at the cemetery. But the places where loving memory may reside are many— the bedroom of the person who has died, the house that held so many memories of the person, the place where they were last seen by search parties, or the automobile crash site. All of these physical places represent sites of the heart.

In each of these places our relationships continue. When we remember, visit, sweep a tomb, place flowers, or light a candle, we do as we have always done for the other—we give. And those who perform these silent acts know what these sacred places give back to them.

They return simple messages of need—as when the candle needs re-lighting, the flowers replacing, or the tomb another sweep. In the act of remembrance, in giving and receiving again, we mirror the love we have for the one who died.

Time does not heal all wounds. This is because grief over the loss of a much-loved human being is not a wound but a changed relationship. We stand interminably on the edge of this new relationship searching and yearning for the old one. We miss the person who has left us and it is a deep, never-ending kind of missing. We keep our heart-fires alive, no matter what others think, hopeful that the subject of our love and attention can see those eternal flames inside us. By our soulful acts of remembrance, at places significant only to us, we call that person back into our arms. We beckon to the white butterfly.

# 33

# Death Pact

℘℘℘

At a conference some time ago in Washington DC, I caught up with my old friend Carl, an academic and counselor who, although American, works permanently in Japan. I took the opportunity to ask him about a small problem that had been brought to me by a Japanese relative. I told Carl my story this way.

My mother's cousin was very close to her mother. They had made a pact between them that if one should die before the other, the dead person would attempt to visit the other to assure them of their continued existence. A year or two passed, and quite suddenly the mother died.

When I heard this story from the lips of my mother's cousin, her mother had been dead for two years. The question she posed was: why had she not heard from her mother? A tear appeared on her downcast face as she asked me more questions. Did this silence mean that her mother did not survive? Or did it mean that her mother did not care and had abandoned the pact? Was her mother in difficulties?

I talked possibilities. Maybe death was something like other forms of travel where contacting home could be more difficult than you think; or maybe her mother had contacted her, but she had not noticed. Behind the maybes was the unspoken understanding that her mother had not survived after all. Maybe.

I took this experience away with me feeling that I had handled the question poorly. I asked my American friend what he would have done in my shoes. Carl is a gentle and thoughtful man, someone used to discussing the undiscussable with the Japanese. He answered my question readily, as he had answered such questions many times before. He simply replied that when people asked him these questions he asked them another, "Are you absolutely sure that you have not heard from them? Think carefully. Are you sure?"

How many times is the obvious not obvious? Remember when you have searched the house for your car keys only to find them somewhere that you thought you had searched before? How many times have I seen my partner search for her glasses when they were sitting on the ridge of her nose? Why am I so often accused of "domestic blindness" by my partner when looking for kitchen things that she finds at the very spot I seem to be gazing? How much more is the obvious not obvious when you become frantic, hysterical, or stricken with grief?

Sometimes you need to go over your life since the death of someone you love, reflecting on the times when you have been alone, or remembering the dreams that you have had since that time. I have listened to people who told me that their "dead" daughter had visited them in a dream or that strange and inexplicable events had happened at home which they connected to the person who had passed away.

When I worked in a hospital melanoma unit, the small staff there related such a story. They had been caring for a young man with advanced melanoma. In his twenties, he had few interests in his life except for an obsession with reptiles. This particularly irked the female nursing staff of the unit. He once even brought to the unit some large lizards in a jar and proudly showed them off.

Some days after this man died, several staff noticed a large lizard crawling slowly up the wall inside the melanoma unit. No one had ever sighted a reptile of any sort on the hospital grounds let alone inside the unit. This was unprecedented and everyone was surprised. The proximity of this event so close to the man's death was not lost on staff who were left to ponder the connection. Yes, it might be a coincidence, but what an interesting one.

You can make meaning out of anything. When I was a child, I used to love to begin my drawings from random squiggles and marks on a piece of paper. There is a fine line between self-delusion and personal meaning, for sure, but never let others decide for you. Only you know who loves you. And some love letters are, and will always be, in secret code. Some messages will be for your eyes only. Even in death.

# 34

# Folly

ഇരു

When I was seven, I met a woman named Folly. She was a widow of sixty something. When she was forty, her husband died of cardiac failure. She never remarried and every year, on the anniversary of her husband's death, I would find Folly quietly weeping in her sunroom. She never got over that death. Apart from me, the only other people who mattered in her life were her two sons. One later died of a heart attack, and his son, Folly's grandson, was killed in the Vietnam war. Each one of these deaths was a sword into her heart. She cried terrible tears.

Folly saw her life as luckless. She often said that she wished she had died instead of her husband, or her son, or her grandson. And I had no doubt that she meant it. She often asked, 'Why them?' And I would ask just as often, "Why her?"

As each summer gave way to the next, Folly and I would spend weekends in her garden, defending the coleus against the snails or her carnations against fellow pensioners who came in the night to snip a flower or two. We fought the good fight against her garden's immortal weeds. And during our weeding, and between feeding the chickens and the pulling up of carrots for her Sunday roast, she would confide in me about her fears. The biggest one was the prospect of losing her independence. She had to stay at home. Couldn't live without the garden or her dogs Tippy and Tiny. Their tails would swing about on hearing their names as we all sat in the dirt together.

But one year Tippy died. And two years later Tiny followed. Somewhere in all these terrible days, Rastus the blue budgie was found dead at the bottom of his cage. And after each death Folly seemed weaker, more tired, and gradually, she took to bed and stayed there. Her only son moved in to care for her. I never knew what was wrong with Folly. When I was at the university I visited her at Christmas and there she was as before—in bed.

Eventually, the worst happened. After battling on for several years Folly and her son decided that she should enter a nursing home. And I never saw her again. I can't tell you when she died, but in any case, I am sure that it was long before she entered the nursing home.

That was the first time that I realized that death was not just a demon that came in the night to take a life, putting a tight, cold hand around the pendulum of our lives. Death wasn't always something inhuman from outside my world. That kind of death took Folly's older son and her grandson. The death that took Folly away was a demon too, but it came for her heart and not the shell that remained as her body. Each grief took her from her garden and from me. I was there and could not stop it. She grabbed at her heart with the news of every loss, but she could not protect it. Folly ebbed away, her eyes looking more distant after each blow. And then, after so much loss, she was gone.

Where did she go? I believe she went into a hiding place that we all have. This is very real, a dark and warm space, where the memories bring back those who have loved us and those we have loved. They are there not as things of today, of course, but as things of substance, all the same. Like our first memories of Christmas tinsel, the smell of sea air, or passionate kisses. They are the deeply comforting things that sustain us. We visit them in reveries on train journeys, or just as we drift into sleep, or when we feel depressed but are trying to look alert at work meetings. Times of dreaming, times of distress.

I don't know what memories made up the world where Folly waited for physical death, but I am sure that Tippy and Tiny were there. I hope that she imagined me there sometimes too. I am not one of those people who "knows" there is life after death or who "knows" that such beliefs are nonsense. When faith deserts me, I cling to my hopes. So I hope that she made it fully into that world before the nursing home people came for her. I hope that she is there now, in a strange and brilliant light that suggests that her companions are much more than mere memory. For her sake and for ours, I hope I am right.

# 35

# Concerning Tears

ℰℭ

In the wet grip of sorrow, I sometimes wonder where tears come from. I know they come from inside me. Although the tears appear to emanate from behind and underneath the eyes, their source is much deeper. They come from hormonal and neurological messages far below and above those eyes. And beyond those ridges, the origin of tears lies even deeper, in the thoughts and feelings that trigger these bodily messenger services, in the ideas that tease and threaten, or experiences that tear away at the soul. Tears come from deep and far-away places within us.

Like the rain, our tears are made by change and turbulence. Tears contribute to the water cycle just as surely as the water cycle has created our life-form and the tears that never seem to end in our personal lives and national histories. When you are sad and cry it is too simple, or simpleminded, to remark that your eyes become wet. You weep, which is to say that you are bent by an experience that is too big for you. The straightness of your spirit has become stooped, you are weighed down, or overwhelmed. You become like a small and lone willow tree.

And the grief comes in waves, without warning. Like eruptions or convulsions there is nothing you can do to prepare for them or stop them. They start out deep within you, like an earthquake emanating from beneath the earth's crust. And when the feeling reaches into your chest and throat, you bend again, racked by yet more tears. As you weep, you place your hand over your eyes, mouth, or face trying to both mop and hide at the same time. The tears taste of salt, something familiar in something so terrible. You feel absolutely awful. You feel so earth-bound, like wet stones and clay and mud. You do not feel like a spirit, like someone with a soul. You feel anything but light. You do not feel like a feather. You do not feel any joy in the sight of flowers. You feel low. You just want to descend to the bowels of the earth and block everything out. Inside that moment, you are the earth.

Even when you feel relatively normal it feels as if there is a hole inside you. Something is missing and nothing can fill it. A sigh can begin another. There is a long, quiet release of breath, a slow draining of the soul. When you say that you miss someone, you really mean that someone has gone missing in your life. You moan for their return, and the moaning and sighing never seem to stop. This vacancy in the heart, this knowledge of loss, is like the sound of your own breath at night. You notice this sound in the dark silence, of air winding in and out of yourself and your sorrow. Amid all this sadness it comes as no surprise how little you absorb when people talk to you.

You hear so much senseless human chatter when all you really want is to regain what you have lost—the whole world can go and be damned really. Away from the talk, when alone, you notice things to which you have never really paid much attention. The wind, for example, winding through the garden and around the house. Its moans communicate to you more clearly than any human counseling. Sometimes the wind hisses and heaves through long grass, or stirs up the dry leaves and then chases them so they run around and around your chair. The wind and your own breathing draw you away from the world, carrying your thoughts and your heart with them on their cold journey to no place.

In sorrow, you are the wind and the rain, and the trees and the earth. The natural world swallows you up and time and again you surrender to this communion. And so the world is not heartless place—a part of life does genuinely stop for your loss. And that part of life is you. You become, in a microcosm, all the things that the universe is. In this small way, in the simple form of you, the earth shows that it truly does mourn for its own.

# 36

# Not Being There

# ∞∞

There are many stories about not being there. There was the man who flew interstate to his dying father but did not make it to his father's bedside in time. There was the family that flew to the bedside of a dying son half way across the world only to discover in their stopover that they were too late. There are countless stories of parents at their dying child's bedside, and children at their dying parent's bedside, who leave that bedside for no more than five minutes to return to find that they have gone. The disbelief, guilt, and anger can be enormous. Parents and children desperately want to be there for each other.

Being there is doing something for another. We often associate just being there as helping bear witness, sharing the ordeal, however remotely. Being there is a spiritual holding of another person's hand, an act of love. So being there for someone you love when they are dying is important in a deeply human and long understood way.

When you are unable to time your arrival to be there for the person you love, the grief you feel can be as deep as it is never-ending. You ask yourself why the dying person could not hold on, wait just a little longer, to give you both that precious extra time. If you were there, but they died when you left the room, the questions about "why" remain. Why did they "choose" to die the very minute you were not there?

Have you ever kept company with a sick or seared child who begged you to stay with them? So you stay, of course, to offer that comfort. When, for whatever good reason, you need to leave briefly—to make coffee, a phone call or to grab a book—you go *after* the child has dozed off. If you have to leave at all, you do it when the child least suspects it. The reason is simple. Leaving when the other person desperately wants you to stay is best done when they have their mind on other things. For that child, sleeping in the dark or feeling sick is bad enough without witnessing a parent leaving.

When dying, the roles can be reversed. Dying is sad enough for everyone but especially for those caring at the bedside who don't want you to leave at all. It is easy to forget that those for whom you care also care about you. At other times, and for other people who are dying, there may be other important reasons for not being there.

There were many times when I did not want my mother by my side despite the fact that I needed all the support I could get. The time that a gang of boys wanted to give me brain damage after a school dance; the day I turned up at a special university hearing to "show cause" why the university should not expel me for failure; the days of despairing grief that followed the death of a favorite dog. There are some things that I need to face alone, and there are other times when I need to be alone.

On those occasions, when the issues I had to face confronted me, I did not love my mother less. I loved my mother unconditionally because that is how I experienced her love. I knew that if I landed up in hospital after the school dance my mother would be the first visitor. She would sit by the bed like a rottweiler guarding her pup. I knew that if the university threw me out, she would help me plan for another future. I knew that she understood that nothing she could say would console my grief for my dog. Leaving me alone would be for the best despite her impulse to do the opposite. Over the years, we both came to know the importance of not being there for each other.

Despite how hard she tried, she did not always understand why she should not be there. But she is not me. My world is not her world. We have both had to learn from each other as best we can, knowing the limits of our common experiences and learning to have faith in each other about the decisions and experiences we cannot share. For both of us, for our own reasons, some journeys have had to be made alone. In these ways, not being there can be a "hands-off" kind of love but, importantly, love all the same. Diversity in the ways of showing care is normal—right up to the last moments of life. Remember that diversity. And remember its source.

# 37

# The First Friend

## ৯৩৫

We met when I was four years old and knew each other until the day he died when I was eleven. We went everywhere together and shared everything. In the summer-times we used to lie on our backs and stare up at the sky. Like generations of young people before us, we tried to work out what shapes the clouds made in their slow journey across the sky. The grass and leaves would stick like paint on his pants and mine as we talked the hot afternoons away to the sounds of cicadas. We climbed trees, built cubby houses out of Queensland box branches laid against pillows of melaleuca shrubbery and hid from our enemies there. We laughed a lot, cried together a little. There were no closer, no better friends than us.

The friends I met at school were never quite the same as him. No one knew how I felt about things more than he did. And when during a despairing fit of temper my mother destroyed him, my grief was inconsolable. Losing my father, my first dog, my house, or my school friends during our many moves could not compare with that loss. Losing my toy rabbit was inexplicably dark and tragic, and I have forgotten neither the times we shared nor his passing.

In the years that I have spent studying death, dying, and loss, I have seen nothing written on this. I have read about the loss of people and limbs, babies and pets, and identity and other parts of the self, but I have never come across a professional story about a boy and his love for his toy rabbit. And I can't understand why this should be.

There is a famous story about a boy and his rabbit called "The Velveteen Rabbit or How Toys Become Real" by Margery Williams, but this is considered children's rather than adult literature.

Every week and every month of my life I notice hundreds of children clutching their toy rabbits and bears. And when these children eventually grow up, do they simply forget their first friend?

Every year, at some barbecue or dinner party, someone will passingly joke about the toy bear or rabbit cherished by their son or daughter. They will tell third-person stories of the near-death experience that Bear had with the washing machine, or the time that Bunny was left behind at the family picnic and they had to double back in the car for an extra and anxious half hour, only to find Bunny sitting up in the grass looking rather cross at the wait. But it's always a joke story, never a love story.

I know that the social rules in life are made by adults, and even those are heated and shaped by the sentiments and priorities of men. In these ways, using those priorities, we can unthinkingly trivialize the relations we have with animals—the dog, cat and horse friends, for example, so important to many of us. The dismay of some people about the grief some people express over the loss of a beloved animal companion is evidence enough of that. And beyond these ridges, lie the loss of other friends that are even more unimaginable for some people. But they are losses.

When I stared into the dark brown glass pupils of my friend (as God is my witness!) I saw the kindest eyes and the most patient face I ever saw. That round white face, like a tenderly misshapen tennis ball with long woolen ears that sat windmill-like across his head, had a look that always made me smile even when I was sad. Can cotton stuffing and wool have so much power over human feelings? Can fabric and glass look back at you, place a warm hand over your heart? I have been there, and I can tell you that the answer to those questions is "yes."

I have thought about this paradox for some years, on and off, on trains, buses and planes, and I think the choices run something like this. Either childhood has a psychotic dimension that involves what the Freudians call "an unconscious projection," or all social relations are imbued with attachment when they occur regularly or are of some personal significance. This might mean that we simply get attached to objects when we have them around us for a long time, become sentimental about them. This may be another way of saying we "project" our feelings on to them, making them "real" in the process. If you believe in psychological explanations, these ideas might have some appeal. I think they are wanting.

What I am telling you is that when my five-year-old eyes met my rabbit's eyes, he looked back at me. What was it I saw? I must insist to you that it was not myself that I saw. And so perhaps there is no answer, as if I saw a UFO and you saw a weather balloon. But then it occurred to me that my rabbit was not the only possession that appeared inanimate and that I related to regularly.

I sing along with my radio, I talk for hours on the phone, and I regularly lose myself in a painting that someone else has painted for me. The wiring and the canvas are go-betweens for a relationship, for the company of beings I cannot see. Maybe my first friend was real, and Bunny was his phone. Or maybe I will never really know.

# 38

# Missing and Hoping

ᔕᗴᑕᗒ

Dante's *The Divine Comedy* begins with a frightening description of the gates of Hell. Over the portals of that gruesome entrance hangs an arch which reads: "All hope abandon, ye who enter here."

When I first read that famous line, I could not think of any slogan more befitting such a place. But I was wrong. There is somewhere worse than Hell and, thousands of people endure it every day. This is the Hell where hope itself is the main instrument of torture and suffering. It is the lot of men and women who lose their loved ones under mysterious circumstances. The person and the love do not return. We see here a new and sad dimension to the age-old problem of unrequited love, and it lies silently among us in every town and city of the modern world.

We think about unrequited love as love that is not returned by the other because they love another person or because there is no genuine mutual feeling. Under these circumstances the person-in-love pines away nonetheless. The birthday of the one you love is remembered. They are in your thoughts daily. And when you go near places where you have met them before, you look for their face in the crowds hoping that you might catch a glimpse of them again.

For many of us who know this situation, another love may take the place of the unrequited one. But sometimes, irrespective of the circumstances, an unrequited love can smolder silently and secretly for years. This is the unrequited love we know. But there is another.

There are famous stories in legend and literature about the unrequited love that is emotionally assured but seems physically lost. There is the Shakespearean tale of Romeo and Juliet where Romeo mistakenly believes that Juliet has taken her life. This belief leads to his suicide which, in turn, leads tragically to hers. The Greek legend of Odysseus describes a warrior and king who leaves his home shores to fight in the Trojan Wars but is kept from returning home for ten years by the god Poseidon. In that time his devoted wife Penelope is bombarded with rumors of Odysseus's death at sea or in battle. The pressure mounts for her to agree to a new suitor, but she resists. Penelope manages to hold out for Odysseus's return, one that few believed was possible after so very long.

These are stories of desperate hope and grief. The personal consequences are always emotionally, and sometimes physically, catastrophic for the one who waits.

Perhaps you are one of them. You may have lost a child or parent. He went off to work one morning, or she went down the street to buy some milk, and was never seen again. Police may suspect abduction and worse. In some countries, it may be the police that you suspect to be involved in your child's disappearance. At other times, your son may have been involved in a war and no one, including his fellow soldiers, ever saw him again. These are the MIA, the people who are missing-in-action. If you care to notice, there are many houses that are home to people whose love has not returned to them. Although the love is assured on both sides, one of them has gone missing, prevented in some way from physically returning.

So you wait. You keep the light on at home at night just in case they return. You keep their favorite foods in the fridge for that wished-for night when they return, a dream dreamt a thousand times. You keep their bedrooms ready, buy new clothes. When shopping or when visiting the place where they were last seen, you search the ground for any small sign of personal belonging, a piece of jewelry or a button. You scan the crowds for their face. You've done these things endless times, like the fisherman who never catches anything in one spot but who casts his line more energetically than the last time in the belief that his success might just be a matter of a few inches away. He strains his arms in the throw; you strain your eyes into the crowds. The desperation and the hope, like the tide itself, rise on each occasion. No doubt more than once you have felt like you were drowning in that tide.

Sometimes, there are public ways of keeping up your strength. Mothers of disappeared children have formed support groups. In Argentina some of these have acted as protest organizations to lobby the government and the military to return their children *alive.* The families of soldiers missing in action have created commemorative times and places for their loved ones. Others have conducted pilgrimages to the sites where their children were last seen. Tombs of the Unknown Soldier have helped to bring some solace, and occasionally, after a long time, perhaps a sense of closure for some.

But for many more there can be no closure, only an endless search for it. Your words seep out from countless homes and nights.

I cannot ask myself or others to abandon the love we hold for one another once I have that love inside me. I can no more give up my arm than release my hope for reunion, or the news or evidence of their certain death. I cannot abandon hope that I might meet once more the person I have lost, even when that hope makes me die just a little every day. I am not comforted by your prayers although I am grateful for them. I hope they might help return to me the person at the center of my loss, or even permit my eyes to notice the sun again. I go to church, but no words come from my lips; my heart stares into the darkness there. There is no rest for me, no words for me, no end for me; sometimes, even, no God for me. I wait for reunion and you cannot help me.

As Dietrich Bonhoeffer has observed, nothing can fill the gap inside me. And it would be wrong for me or anyone else to try. I will hold out because there is nothing else I can do, nothing else I am capable of doing: ". . . It is a nonsense to say that Cod fills the gap; he does not fill it, but keeps it empty so that our communion with another may be kept alive, even at the cost of pain."

# 39

# The Comfort of Darkness

കൃ

Sometimes loss is so painful that you feel a need to *do* something, but what? At an earlier time, a more religious time, some people would go to church when services were not being conducted and just sit in the darkness of that place. We could weep there without anyone noticing. We could take hold of the silence and the darkness and rub both against the soul, attempting to warm a cold grief. We could talk to God, or we could talk to the one we miss and love. We might even do nothing, just sit blankly, using the darkness as a port in the storm of our inner turbulence and sadness. So few of us are religious any more that the church is a difficult place to visit or, for some, a place that may evoke old and unpleasant memories. Even so, many go to these places and tell no one that they do.

The comfort of darkness has long been recognized as a balm for the soul and a place for communication with, or search for, the mysterious disappearance of our attachments. From our dark nightly travels come our dreams. It is also the medium into which we send our prayers, even among those of us who disclaim being dreamers or god-believers. The transition from the visible to the invisible has been a cross-cultural metaphor for the parallel transition from life to death.

Understanding this symbolism, the Chinese have burnt bits of inscribed paper for thousands of years. These contain personal messages or are paper models of houses, furniture and money to send on to their dead. An idea or feeling, which after all is invisible, is transported to the dead via the visible. The burning is the "death" of those paper objects and renders them equally invisible, an enabling process that transports them to their dead loved ones. For similar reasons, both the Chinese and the Japanese use burning incense to send their prayers and wishes to the dead.

In many coastal villages of Japan, around the month of July, people remember their dead in the Three Days of Bon, or the Festival of the Dead. Late at night, small lanterns with wooden bottoms are lit within by a single candle and set free to float away on an outgoing tide. In the fishing village of Yaidzu, the paper lanterns are painted with five colors, each representing the essential elements of life—earth, wind, fire, water, and ether. Under the forgiving cover of darkness, like generations before them, people remember those they have lost. They watch and relive their loss as the little lanterns slowly disappear into the blackness of the night tide.

What does this small light in the darkness, this physical journey of the eye from visible to invisible mean to us?

The early Japanese ethnographer Lafcadio Hearn, a Western man who married a local and lived in Japan most of his life at the turn of the twentieth century, describes an evening during the Three Days of Bon at Yaidzu. On one of these evenings, after everyone had left the shore, Hearn does a striking and unusual thing—he swims out to the colored lanterns, swims among them in the darkness, and alone, reflects on their journey.

What does he see out there alone, among the company of the little glowing lanterns, each departing from him every which-way in the night sea?

In the darkness that envelops the sea, Hearn reflects on how similar these little lanterns are to individual human lives— their frailty, loneliness, beauty, and their final, inevitable dissolution. The quivering of their lights as they bob about the sea conveys a sense of fear about their journey. It once occurs to Hearn that maybe he is not really alone out there. Perhaps someone remains watching. But who is it and what is their purpose?

Hearn's swim among the lanterns, symbolically journeying part way with the souls of Yaidzu, startled me at first. Caught up in the sentiment of the traditional meanings, I initially felt that he had been disrespectful. But later I began to understand that Hearn did what many people do in the comfort of darkness. Like Hearn, we swim out, if not physically, then spiritually, to the souls of our dead for at least part of their journey.

We cannot stop them from going, though God knows we wish that we could. In darkness we can see our dead again, though no words pass between us. Ours is a silent journey. We know that we must return to the light and that they must continue on a path whose destination we can only guess at.

When your loss is great, and your pain even greater, it can be good to visit the dark. Whether it is a quiet church, a desolate beach at night, or the silence of your living room in the early morning, you too can swim among the lanterns. The eyes that watch are your own. And the purpose of the watching is nothing less than to share something together one last time— the silence of each other in the comfort of darkness.

# 40

# To Honor Their Memory

What does honoring the memory of someone mean? One weekend Tony and I decided to make a visit to a cemetery near where we had lived as kids. There were now four of our old friends buried there. We did not have any firm plans about what we wanted to do at that place other than "pay our respects." Neither of us knew exactly what that was. We set off empty-handed.

First, we went to see the gravesite of Doris. Doris was buried with her husband who had "predeceased" her. They were buried in a rectangular plot with a low granite tombstone at the head of the grave. Half of the headstone had her name and dates and the other half bore the inscriptions for her husband. In the middle of the grave lay a wreath holder and protruding from it was a generous bunch of very faded plastic flowers. No one had changed them for some time, maybe even years, so they all looked a pale white with just a tinge of color to hint at their original glory.

Tony and I looked at each other knowingly. We knew that we had to do something about this.

The next visits were to friends who had been cremated. They were in "walls of remembrance." The cemetery computer guide told us that they were at walls 29, 42, and 48 respectively. Each of these walls was low set and built of cream brick about two meters high and five or six meters long. Each contained dozens, perhaps a hundred, small metal plaques slightly bigger than a standard business card. And most of the little metal plaques had a small metal funnel attached to them, something to hold a single flower stem. We first stopped at Yoshiko's plaque. We immediately noticed that the flower holder had broken away and was entirely missing.

Tony and I glanced at each other with a slightly pained look.

We then moved to Robbo's plaque. It was intact, but the black writing had faded in parts.

This was too much for Tony who declared his disappointment and anxiety about the damage in a hurt voice. He noted how the other plaques did not seem to have this problem. He observed the fallen bark and leaves and told me that old Robbo hated trees. Other people's trees had condemned him to raking leaves forever in his backyard.

Finally, we moved to Denis's plaque. It was intact as was the black type. But there was no flower in his holder.

We stood there quietly. My hands played with an over-hanging branch of bush, and I toyed with breaking a bit off to put in Denis's holder, but could not decide.

"Euonium," said Tony in a low voice.

"Yes," I said mindlessly, "the ladybird beetles like them."

After a minute we left. Tony and I were anguished at the thought of any of the plaques or graves being damaged in any way; of the flowers not being bright or fresh; even the vision of a plaque that had no flowers.

We both know that our dead are *not* here. But our memories *are* prompted here, and the symbols of their former lives *are* here. In these ways, they *are* here. And any slight to these physical reminders is a slight to our hearts. And we are hurt by them. We resolve to fix the plaques and bring flowers when we return.

Later I am at an editorial board meeting for a journal that deals principally with HIV/AIDS issues. There is discussion that we should change the journal's name to reflect that much of the research we do now is as much about hepatitis C and injecting drug use as HIV contracted through sex. The discussion goes well, and we have almost settled on a new name for the journal which relegates the acronym HIV to a subtitle. Someone interjects at the last moment.

He speaks quietly, movingly. The board, the journal and the funding for both, he observes, stem from the initial work of two people who are now dead. Both were people who had later died of AIDS. The editorial board and the journal, he adds, were founded on the original problem, which still exists, of HIV/AIDS. To "demote" this disease from our titles is to also "demote" the work and memory of these workers. We all watch this speaker, observe his eyes moisten as he compassionately presents another form of reasoning, and does so lovingly, about those people and their work.

I don't know what the others are thinking, but I think about the faded plastic flowers, a broken flower holder, and some missing black type on our friends' plaques at the cemetery some miles from where this discussion is happening. I feel the others are making their own connections. All of us know this is probably not important to our dead. We know that the journal is not a memorial device but an academic one.

On the other hand, we know that honoring the memory of those who have given what precious time they had left to the establishment of the journal was a life and death matter for them. They worked to contribute to a cause that might prevent others from dying. We saw that none of us want anything to do with decision-making that does not recognize the real humanity behind it. We restore HIV to the title. No questions.

So much of what we do we do for others. You buy a coffee for a friend. You write a reference for another. You straighten the tie of a colleague who is about to go for a job interview. You wish them luck. And when they die, you don't stop caring. The sites of care move. We take flowers.

We ask others to remember in tangible ways. We remind others not to forget in the medical research we do, or in the poems we write about each other, or in the outrage we feel at every Aboriginal death in custody, or every child who dies in neglect. In all these ways, we reach down and connect to the ones we love who are not around any more.

What does it mean to honor the memory of our dead? It means to care about what happens to them as if they were not dead. And it means to care for these others as if we had been given a second chance. Honoring our dead is honoring life—theirs and ours, seen and unseen.

# Parting Words

# At Day's End

ℰℭ

Remember Mee? Arthur Mee was that English children's editor with an optimism for life and a faith in God and the human spirit. At seventy, he developed a mysterious illness that required urgent surgery. In keeping with the style of the times, his 1940s biographer did not tell us the nature of this medical condition. Unlike our obsessions with medical categories today, he didn't feel the need to name the illness.

In the end, as always, it doesn't matter. One morning, Arthur entered the hospital to have the necessary surgery but did not survive it. I will always remember his marvelous book, which I wrote about earlier, called *Arthur Mee's Book of Everlasting Things*. I found my copy in a book section of an old trash and treasure market in London. And treasure it is. I wish you the same luck some day.

The last example of an everlasting thing that Mee presented us with was a poem. It was on the last page of his everlasting book, and it was written by Joseph the hymnographer "a thousand years ago" and translated by J. M. Neale. Time will tell us whether Arthur and his friend Joseph are right. Like Arthur Mee, we can only wonder. And hope.

> Safe home, safe home in port;
> Strained cordage, shattered deck,
> Tom sail, provisions short,
> And only not a wreck;
> But, oh, the joy, upon the shore
> To tell our voyage perils o'er!
>
> The prize, the prize secure!
> The wrestler nearly fell;
> Bore all he could endure
> And bore not always well;
> But he may smile at troubles gone
> Who sets the victor's garland on.
>
> The exile is at home;
> O nights and days of tears!
> O longings not to roam!
> O sins and doubts and fears!
> What matters now? O joyful day!
> The King hath wiped all tears away!

# Index

෨෬

Abuhene (god of death), 113
Accept your lot in life, refusing
    to, 36–37
Accident victims, perceptions of,
    23–25
Adam and Eve and the Tree of
    Knowledge, 4, 5
Adversity creating grounds for
    improvement, 31–34
Aeschylus, 129
African-Americans and,
    associating blackness with
    evil, 85–86
Afterlife, questions about the,
    15–17
Agency (control over life), 36–37
Animal companions, 152
Answers about death, few ready,
    90–92
*Arabian Nights,* xx–xxi, xxii
Architecture, inspirational,
    101–102

Babies leaving a legacy, 48–49
Beautiful, people who view death
    as, 90
Being there/not being there,
    147–149
Bible, the, 4–5, 16, 105–108
Big brother/sister mode when
    confronted with sick
    individuals, 94–95
Blackness, associating death
    with, 85–86
Blake, William, 101
Bohemia, 113
Bonhoeffer, Dietrich, 158
*Book of Everlasting Things, The*
    (Mee), 80, 169–170
Burning to send prayers/wishes
    to the dead, 160–161

Castaways, 99
Cemeteries, 163–165

# About the Author

ℰ∂∽∾ℭℛ

Allan Kellehear was born and educated in Sydney, Australia and is Professor of Palliative Care at La Trobe University in Melbourne; he received his Ph.D. in sociology from the University of New South Wales in Sydney. He was British Academy Visiting Professor at the University of Bath, England, in 2000 and Visiting Professor of Australian Studies at the University of Tokyo in 2003-2004. Dr. Kellehear is also Professorial Fellow in the Department of General Practice at the University of Melbourne Medical School, chairman of the Scientific Advisory Committee of the National Center for HIV Social Research, and (in 2002-2003) chairman of the Board of Palliative Care Victoria. He is the author or editor of 17 books, including, *Health Promoting Palliative Care,* and *Experiences near Death.*